ESSENTIALS OF ART THERAPY
EDUCATION AND PRACTICE

ABOUT THE AUTHOR

Bruce L. Moon is an artist and art therapist with extensive clinical, teaching, and administrative experience. He is a registered and board-certified art therapist who holds a doctorate in creative arts with specialization in art therapy. Bruce is the Director of the Graduate Art Therapy program at Mount Mary College in Milwaukee. His clinical practice of art therapy, focused on the treatment of emotionally disturbed children, adolescents, and adults, has spanned over 25 years. He has lectured and led workshops at many colleges and universities in the United States and Canada.

Bruce is the author of *Existential Art Therapy: The Canvas Mirror; Introduction to Art Therapy: Faith in the Product; Art and Soul: Reflections on an Artistic Psychology; The Dynamics of Art as Therapy with Adolescents; Ethical Issues in Art Therapy;* and *Working with Images: The Art of Art Therapists.* He has also written a number of journal articles. Bruce brings to this second edition of *Essentials of Art Therapy Education and Practice* many years of experience in art studios, clinical settings, and educational settings. His educational background integrates a rich tradition of interdisciplinary training in theology, art therapy, education, and visual art. He is an active painter, songwriter, and performer.

On the cover: Photograph taken by Lisa Hinkle.

Second Edition

ESSENTIALS OF ART THERAPY EDUCATION AND PRACTICE

By

BRUCE L. MOON, PH.D., ATR-BC

With a Foreword by

James Lantz, PH.D.

And an Introduction by

Catherine Moon, MA, ATR-BC

CHARLES C THOMAS • PUBLISHER, LTD.
Springfield • Illinois • U.S.A.

Published and Distributed Throughout the World by

CHARLES C THOMAS • PUBLISHER, LTD.
2600 South First Street
Springfield, Illinois 62794-9265

©2003 by CHARLES C THOMAS • PUBLISHER, LTD.

ISBN 0-398-07391-0 (hard)
ISBN 0-398-07392-9 (paper)

Library of Congress Catalog Card Number: 2002043125

Printed in the United States of America
MM-R-3

Library of Congress Cataloging in Publication Data

Moon, Bruce, L.
    Essentials of art therapy education and practice / by Bruce L. Moon;
with a foreword by James Lantz and an introduction by Catherine
Moon. -- 2nd ed.
        p. cm.
    Includes bibliographical references and index.
    ISBN 0-398-07391-0 (hc.) -- ISBN 0-398-07392-9 (pbk.)
    1. Art therapy--Study and teaching. 2. Art therapy--Methodology.
    I. Title.

RC489.A7 M659 2003
615.8'5156--dc21   2002043125

FOREWORD

Bruce Moon is an artist, a psychotherapist, an art therapist, and a teacher of existential art therapy. Moon challenges the common attitude that the psychotherapist should be trained to be a technical practitioner whose interpretations are based upon cookbook prescriptions that are designed to confront psychopathology or maladaptive behavior, without understanding the personhood of the one who comes in pain to ask for the therapist's help.

Central to Moon's approach is the manner in which the mentor and the beginning art therapist come together in their efforts to learn and grow. Moon demonstrates the deep, intimate, alive, and complex training relationship that can lead to the awareness of meaning in the lives of both. The concern for authentic engagement in the training relationship enhances the beginner's ability to use the *self* to help clients learn to use art and artistic expression to identify and integrate new insights in their lives.

Bruce's excellent book is ultimately concerned with the use of art and the artistic relationship to promote human growth. His deep understanding of both art and existentialism makes this book a high point in the ever-evolving fields of existential psychotherapy and art therapy. It is an important contribution to the development of creative, effective psychotherapists who value human growth and who refuse to slide into the dehumanizing trends of modern society. I highly recommend this book for those who are interested in art, art therapy, existential psychotherapy, and the development of a future generation of psychotherapists who will dare to be creative, continuing to cherish the caring core of the helping process.

JIM LANTZ, PH.D.
Ohio State University
Worthington Logotherapy Center

Author's Note

The clinical accounts in this book are in spirit true. In all instances, however, names have been changed and identifying information regarding clients has been so obscured as to insure the privacy and confidentiality of the persons with whom I have worked.

The case illustrations presented are amalgamations of many specific situations. Factual data has been fictionalized in order to protect the individual.

INTRODUCTION

At the close of one chapter in this book, Bruce Moon says, "Attend to your passions. If you have lost the zeal that once powered your journey, return to the studio, for it is there that you first stumbled upon the power of images and art processes." If there is one essential element to this book on the essentials of art therapy, it is Bruce's belief in art as the core of our profession. He does not suggest that we value *art* above *therapy*, but rather that to be an art therapist means there is no way to tease out one from the other. An art therapist who is "passionately disciplined" is willing to plunge into the dark depths of the soul and use what is found there as the very stuff of his or her art making. It is this fierce faith in the process of art making that undergirds our profession. This is what, at the most essential level, we art therapists bring to the client-therapist and educator-student relationships.

With this "passionate discipline" as the warp that holds together the weft of his book, Bruce goes on to enumerate the various elements necessary for the training and practice of art therapists. His experience as an artist/clinician/educator gives the book credibility. He is not speaking theoretically about the necessary intertwining of these disciplines. He speaks with the voice of one actively engaged in these three aspects of art therapy. So it is that he can make assertions such as:

> Educators of art therapists must resist the seduction of training their students to be *as-if* psychologists or pseudo-counselors.
>
> Students who want to become art therapists must insist that they be educated as art therapists and nothing less.
>
> If we abandon the art process for ourselves, we art therapists will eventually dry up and be blown away like dust.

Although you, as reader, may not agree with all that Bruce writes, his words are likely to engender a response in you. His writing is clearly born of passionate conviction and the authority of lived experience. For this reason, what you read in this book may at times comfort, at times irritate, at times challenge, and at times inspire you.

I think Bruce would say this is how it must be. It is not easy to be an art therapist, to be passionately disciplined. It is comforting, irritating, challenging, inspiring work. Bruce writes, "The work of the artist is not easy, covered with blisters both physical and emotional, tired muscles, cramped fingers, and weary eyes. The work of an artist is a testament to faith that the struggle is worth it, that it mattered." If we art therapists bring this kind of faith and conviction to our work as educators and therapists, the students and clients we work with are sure to reap the benefits.

CATHERINE MOON, MA, ATR-BC

PREFACE

During my career, I worked for 22 years as an art therapist at Harding Hospital, in Worthington, Ohio and as the co-director of the Harding Graduate Clinical Art Therapy Internship Program. I have provided clinical services to thousands of clients and educational services to hundreds of students. For the past several years, my work has been focused on art therapy education and, to a lesser degree, private practice.

Currently I am the director of the Mount Mary College graduate art therapy program and an associate professor. I am in the unique position of being an educator who has: (1) been an on-site supervisor to art therapy practicum students, (2) served as a clinical program director, (3) provided art therapy clinical services in institutions and in private practice, and (4) written about art therapy theory. Through these different responsibilities, I've had many opportunities to observe and influence educational processes. I hope this second edition of Essentials of Art Therapy Education and Practice will offer another chance to encourage and inspire future art therapists.

The title of this book, *ESSENTIALS OF ART THERAPY EDUCATION AND PRACTICE,* reflects my efforts to explore the crucial components of the education of creative arts therapists. The first edition of this book was born of my desire to describe what my colleagues and I do as we integrate the complex fields of art, therapy, and education. Since its publication in 1992, there have been significant developments in the profession of art therapy, important modifications in the educational standards of the American Art Therapy Association, and profound changes in health care. In this second edition, I update specific portions of the book to reflect these changes and attempt to articulate the elements of art therapy and art therapy education that are essential to helping students become knowledgeable and skilled therapists. I originally conceived of this book as being written for art therapy educators and supervisors, but have come to see the benefits it can offer to students and seasoned practitioners as well.

Art therapy educators are keenly aware that our success or lack of success with educating our students will one day affect the lives of clients who come to them seeking help. Thus educators have an important responsibility to students and future clients alike. I hope this book adds to our development as a profession.

Over the past 28 years, I have worked with clients through music, drama, creative writing, and sculpture, but it is in painting and drawing that I feel most comfortable. I hope that readers who specialize in other media will forgive me for sharing clinical vignettes that primarily feature drawing. While I embrace and appreciate the use of all of the creative arts, I am most at home in the visual medium.

In writing, I have drawn from the experiences of experts in the field of art therapy education: art therapy students. I have asked them to teach me and I am grateful that they have been willing to do so. Their candor has allowed me to get as close to their experience as possible. They have even allowed portions of their daily journals to be shared here. Much of this book is also built around my interactions with the students I have taught and supervised. Without the contributions of students over the years, my understanding of the essentials of art therapy training would never have taken form.

This book is also about the practice of art therapy and the essential role art making plays in both practice and education. It is impossible to write about educating art therapists without reference to the clinical and artistic work that students are in training to do. Likewise, it would be difficult to write about the practice of art therapy without regard to the educational and artistic experiences that precede it. These subjects are tightly interwoven.

BRUCE L. MOON

ACKNOWLEDGMENTS

I am indebted to many people who have, in their ways, contributed to the writing of the second edition of this book. Perhaps most important are the students and clients I've come to know these past 27 years. They are truly the ones who taught me most of what I believe to be essential in art therapy training and practice.

Special thanks go to Ellie Jones, the editor of the first edition of this book. Ellie and Cathy Moon made significant editorial suggestions for this second edition and I am deeply appreciative of their efforts. Ellie worked wonders, smoothing and trimming my sometimes-awkward presentation. By working with Ellie and Cathy I have learned to write coherent sentences.

Thanks also go to the contributors to this work, Jim Lantz, Cathy Moon, Joan Selle (now Joan Zeller), and Lou Powers. Debra DeBrular, a cherished colleague, also made significant offerings to this book. I am forever grateful, Deb.

For 22 years, I was deeply affected by creative, conflicted, painful, and pleasurable encounters with my former colleagues at Harding Hospital. They were interested in my work and encouraged me to pursue putting my ideas into words. Most important, they gave me time to write.

I've also been fortunate to work in very supportive academic settings. My colleagues at Marywood University in Scranton, Pennsylvania, and at Mount Mary College in Milwaukee have challenged my ideas, sharpened insights, and helped to sustain my efforts. I am thankful.

B.L.M.

CONTENTS

Page

Foreword by James Lantz v
Introduction by Catherine Moon vii
Preface ix

Chapter
    I.   The Image 3
    II. Making Art 11
   III. Beginnings 20
   IV. Beginner's Chaos 30
    V. The Journey Metaphor in Education 37
   VI. The Mentor Supervisor 42
  VII. The Art Experience 53
 VIII. The Core Curriculum 59
   IX. The Practical Experience 66
    X. Science and Soul in the Clinical Setting 77
   XI. The Work of Art Therapy 81
  XII. The Young Student 86
 XIII. Gifts of the Female and Male Student 93
 XIV. The Role of Philosophy 108
  XV. Therapy and Holidays 117
 XVI. Metaverbal Therapy 122
 XVII. The Mirror 130
XVIII. The Role of Metaphor 137
 XIX. The Role of Love 142
  XX. The Role of Assessment 148
 XXI. The Role of Work 163
 XXII. Painting My Way Home 168

Epilogue 175
Index 177

LIST OF FIGURES

Page

Photo of the Author *by Cathy Moon* ii
Figure 1. Two Women–Acrylic on paper *by Cathy Moon* 5
Figure 2. The Spot 7
Figure 3. Untitled–Acrylic on board *by Cathy Moon* 9
Figure 4. Lou Powers Studio 12
Figure 5. Lou Powers 24
Figure 6. Scribble–Pastel chalk on brown paper 31
Figure 7. Outside the Studio at Harding Hospital 35
Figure 8. Chalk Woman–Pastel chalk on brown paper 36
Figure 9. The Quest–Mixed media on paper .38
Figure 10. Dangerous Place - Acrylic on canvas 41
Figure 11. Mentor 44
Figure 12. Waiting–Oil Stik 49
Figure 13. My Studio 55
Figure 14. On the Corner–Acrylic on canvas .57
Figure 15. The Tool Shed–Acrylic on canvas .58
Figure 16. Communion–Acrylic on canvas 62
Figure 17. Communion # 2–Acrylic on canvas 64
Figure 18. Olives–Oil on masonite board 70
Figure 19. Where–Mixed media on canvas 71
Figure 20. Morning–Oil stik on canvas 72
Figure 21. Heart Lines–Mixed media on canvas 74
Figure 22. Feed Them–Oil stik on wood panel 75
Figure 23. Panorama–Oil stik on canvas 79
Figure 24. Working in the studio–Photograph 85
Figure 25. Male and Female–Chalk on paper 95
Figure 26. It Is Late–Acrylic on canvas 98
Figure 27. Self Bowl–Oil stik on canvas 106
Figure 28. Communion–Acrylic on canvas 114
Figure 29. The Mirror 132
Figure 30. Red Cup 140

Figure 31.   Cathy and Brea–Photograph 152
Figure 32.   Digging in the dirt–Photograph 165
Figure 33.   129 Piper Street–Oil on canvas 170
Figure 34.   129 Piper Street–detail #1 171
Figure 35.   129 Piper Street–detail #2 172

ESSENTIALS OF ART THERAPY EDUCATION AND PRACTICE

Chapter I

THE IMAGE

The First Essential—We regard images as living entities.

Images and metaphors present themselves always as living
psychic subjects with which I am obliged to be in relation . . .
A particular image is a necessary angel waiting for a response.
How we greet this angel will depend on our sensitivity to its
reality and presence.

James Hillman, *The Blue Fire*

Those who will not slip beneath
    the still surface on the well of grief
turning downward through its black water
    to the place we cannot breathe
will never know the source from which we drink
    the secret water, cold and clear,
nor find in the darkness glimmering
    the small round coins
thrown by those who wished for something else

David Whyte, *Where Many Rivers Meet*

Let us turn our attention to the place of *the image* in our profession. Although absolutely central to the existence of the creative arts therapies, image has received less attention in published works than one would expect. Authors seem comfortable describing art processes, art-making materials and tools, and, of course, therapeutic strategies. However, the image has received relatively little press. When I speak of image in this context, I am referring to the inner visualized form that emerges within an individual's imagination. When image has taken center stage, it has often been in the service of a fixed psychological scheme or theory of explanation. This does not, in my view, give images their proper respect. Image has been pressed, pounded, or poured into intellectual frameworks of understanding generally related to interpretation. From such efforts come interpretive equations

3

such as *that* means *that*, or *this* equals *this*. Invariably these cookbook interpretive formulas focus on specific images as indicative of pathology or illness, leading to a rather sick view of imagery. Such interpretive equations become popular because they reduce or eliminate ambiguity and give the pretense of precision. For example, if a particular interpretive formula suggests that images of caves are indicative of issues related to feminine sensuality, then there is no mystery, no uncertainty or vagueness about the meaning of the image. Thus, when an art therapist who embraces such systems of interpretation encounters an image of a cave, she immediately "knows" the issues the client is struggling with.

I hope that readers of this text will abandon all hope of arriving at a systematic, verifiable formula for understanding images. In Moon (1990, 1995), I coined the term *imagicide*, the killing of image. As art therapists, we must avoid external pressures that would turn us into imagicidal practitioners. McNiff (1991) refers to images as autonomous entities. The first essential aspect of the arts therapies is that images are regarded as living things. Whatever the form–the words of the poet, the tones of the musician, the brushstrokes of the painter or the fleeting gestures of the dancer–the image has life (Fig. 1).

In the early years of my career, influenced by the ideas of Picasso, I often asserted that all things we create are self-portraits. As my work has evolved, I've found it necessary to amend this view. I still contend that all things I create are at least a partial self-portrait, but I now know that there is more to the image than just me.

In a lecture to the students of the Harding Graduate Clinical Art Therapy Program, Shaun McNiff used the metaphor of children to demonstrate this point. While certainly our children reflect characteristics of their parents, he insisted, children are *not* their parents. "They have a life of their own" (McNiff, 1992). My children have certainly confirmed that McNiff is correct in this assertion.

I have often referred to H. W. Janson's (1973) description of art making as a birth process (p. 10). So, if the image I release upon the canvas may be likened to my child, I am forced to modify my previous conviction that it is no more than a portrait of me. My real-life children remind me constantly that they are not me. When I look at the images in my art, I am confronted with this same reality. I must speak to my painting respectfully, regarding it both as a part of me, and yet, not me.

Figure 1. The image has life.

The notion that an image has a life of its own and its own stories to tell can be demonstrated at an art exhibit. If the viewers of any piece are asked to tell the story of the work, it is intriguing what will emerge! No two stories are exactly the same.

I admire the work of Edward Hopper and one of my favorites is his painting, *Nighthawks*. I have not read a description by Hopper of his intent with this painting. I have actually avoided doing so. The stories this image tells me are far more interesting to me than any he may have written or spoken of. The painting has a life of its own, separate and distinct from that of Edward Hopper. To be sure, it may represent some facets of Hopper the man, but it represents itself to me without my having knowledge of Hopper's personality or biography. According to Hillman (1989), it is a necessary angel awaiting my response to its message (pp. 50–70).

In April of 1991, I was a presenter at the Midwestern Illinois Arts Therapy Conference hosted by Jerilee Cain, Ph.D., at Western Illinois

University. The keynote speaker was David Whyte, a poet from the Pacific northwest. During his presentation, he recited his poem, *The Well of Grief.* As his resonant voice rose and said, ". . . in the darkness glimmering, the small round coins thrown by those who wished for something else," I was caught up in wonder. I have no idea what Whyte intended with these words, what personal pain or loss they might represent, but when I read them, I have a very clear image of myself lying deep in the murky well waters as the shiny slivers of another's wishes tumble past. I recall the faces of grief I have known. I remember the tugging, gnawing, longing to be on the surface, away from my own mourning. David Whyte's image, ". . . glimmering, the small round coins . . .," becomes my image. A necessary angel, it waits for my response. It will not leave me alone. It calls me into dialogue. I speak with the image and it teaches me, not only about David Whyte, but about myself as well.

To regard the image as being greater than, or more than, a reflection of the self who created it requires a willingness to let go. I can best explain this by referring to my own artwork. The painting in Figure 2 is of the little cafe in my hometown where my friends and I gathered throughout my adolescence. I painted it during a period of intense reflection and introspection about my past. It is one of a series of paintings with similar themes, that is, scenes of my childhood. When I look at this painting, I can smell the hamburgers and fries. I can hear the laughter of my buddies. I remember standing on the corner, heartbroken after breaking up with my girlfriend. I remember the feel of sitting in the 1965 VW beetle that is parked alongside the building.

These memories and sensations are rich and meaningful for me. However, when I exhibited the painting in the Harding Hospital auditorium, I was fascinated by the comments others made about it. Each viewer made up his or her own story to fit the scene. Of course, none of their stories matched my own. There was a moment of artist-indignation as I eavesdropped on others' reactions to the work, but it became clear that the stories others told about this image had some personal meaning to the storyteller. My painting called them into a dialogue that was different from the one I experienced. I began to understand the meaning of letting go. I could not control how the image conversed with someone else. The image asserted its own existence. Had I intervened and said, "No, you misunderstand . . . this painting is about . . ." I would have committed imagicide (and perhaps

Figure 2. Each viewer made up his or her own story to fit the scene.

symbolic infanticide as well). All I could do was let go.

Catherine Moon describes this process of hearing others dialogue with her images as like trying on someone else's perspective. It is instructive, for it deepens and expands the artist's own dialogue with the work (Fig. 3).

Those who embrace a psychoanalytic theoretical framework might classify these encounters as *projections*. I do not object to this term if projection is seen as the cornerstone of empathy and not as a building block of pathology. Ultimately, it is the ability of the creative arts therapist to project himself or herself into the image of the client that lays the groundwork for the establishment of a therapeutic relationship. It can be argued that all good relationships are formed through disciplined acknowledgment of and willingness to work with projective experiences. It could be formulized as follows: I project upon you, you project upon me, and then we attempt to make sensible meaning out of the process.

This is a possible description of the interaction among the creative arts therapist, the artist/client, and the image before them. The image is the intermediary. It is not only an object-thing to be used as the basis of client revelatory conversation. It is a subject capable of teaching both client and therapist about themselves and one another.

It is helpful to think of art therapy relationships as being comprised of three equal partners: the client, the artwork, and the art therapist. When there is dialogue among these three partners, the rights of all are respected. Having compassion for images and regarding them as independent entities, separate and distinct from the persons who made them, opens possibilities for how we think and talk about what we do in art therapy. It also opens us to ways of behaving toward our clients and their artworks. These ways of thinking and acting foster relationships that are respectful, empathic and deeply therapeutic.

If one regards images as autonomous, separate entities, one begins to view them as sacred, living things. As arts therapists, then, we are those who attend to living images as well as to the living persons who made them.

Kirkegaard (1956) touches on such a perspective as he discusses devotional listening. "In a devotional sense . . . to listen in order to act, this is the highest thing of all" (p. 179). I propose that we art therapists adopt the phrase *devotional seeing*. To see in order to act (the action being the attending to the client artist) is devotional seeing.

Hyperattention to pathology has had a damaging impact upon our ability to regard images and their creators as entities worthy of our respect. From a pathological perspective, it is possible to view images as signposts of disease, and artist-clients as diagnostic categories or symptom clusters. Yet images need not simply be objects of analytical inquiry. They can also be subjects capable of teaching. If the image has a life of its own, with its own purpose, then we who involve ourselves with the image must regard our work as sacred. As art therapists, we deal with living images and the living artists who made them. Both subjects command deep respect.

If we regard images as having lives of their own, it is impossible to establish any formula for interpretation or equation for analysis. In art therapy relationships, the reality is that *this* does not always mean *that*. In my work with clients' images, I resist the urge to see images as specimens to be dissected, measured, and classified or diagnosed. I believe it is much healthier for art therapists, clients, and image to embrace the mystery of creation and cultivate devotional seeing.

We have the option of handling our clients' images, and our own, as infectious and diseased, or as living things worthy of our most tender care and highest respect. How we regard images colors every aspect of our career. It affects how we relate to our artist/clients, our colleagues, and ourselves. I urge compassion and empathy over dissection and imagicide.

Images are not concrete. Images will always be ambiguous, precocious, and subject to change. The world of imagery is full of shadow

Figure 3. It deepens and expands the artists own dialogue.

and mist, a spectrum of gray areas. Embrace the mystery. Dedicate yourself to devotional seeing and constant exploration in a world where nothing is sure.

The place of the image in the creative arts therapy professions is at the center–the heart. Enjoy your clumsy, stammering, stumbling attempts at dialogue. This is the essential nature of what we art therapists do.

Chapter II

MAKING ART

The Second Essential–Art therapists make art.

Why do I make art? Why do you make art? Should art therapists be actively involved in making their own art? There may be no more important questions for art therapists to ask themselves. Why make art?

Painting, sculpting, and dancing are very different activities from *talking* about painting, sculpting, and dancing. In order to be an art therapist, one must be an artist. Art is the anchor, the heart and the taproot of the profession. Allen (1992) noted, "art therapists have a right and even a responsibility to make art at their placements during training and subsequently at their jobs" (p. 28). It is the process of making art, particularly in the clinical employment context, that one's identity as a therapeutic artist is forged (Fig. 4).

Why should art therapists make art?

As I have been thinking about this essential question, a number of compelling answers have occurred to me. I believe personal art making serves several functions for the art therapist. Personal art making provides: (1) a mechanism to clarify, express, and contain the art therapist's feelings that surface in therapeutic work; (2) a form of exploration and documentation of therapeutic work; (3) a basis for responsive interaction with clients; (4) a kind of spiritual practice, or participation in soul-making; and (5) the basis of authentic relationship with self and others.

Art Making as a Form of Clarification, Expression, and Containment of Feelings

It is not easy to make art. I often begin my artwork in the midst of turmoil, whether painful, or joyous, or frightening life events. The circumstances that lead me to make art are diverse, but my work is often

Figure 4. Why art therapists make art.

inspired by, or in reaction to, my work as a therapist. It is impossible to be in the company of clients who are struggling with potent emotional issues and not be affected. There are some common threads in my paintings that appear time and again. Prominent themes that emerge revolve around my awareness of my freedom, aloneness, guilt, sense of responsibility for my life, the inevitability of struggle and death, and a deep longing for meaning.

The arts have always dealt with the ultimate concerns of existence and it is because of this tradition that I make art. Every time I fill my brush and move it across the canvas I am declaring to the world, "I am! I exist!"

My work as a painter is all about wrestling with the anxiety that forms in response to an awareness of these ultimate concerns of life. My images are tied to the creative struggle (my own and my clients) with the core issues of meaning, isolation, freedom, and death. A primary source of my creative work is my own turmoil brought on by the struggle with the ultimate concerns. Art making has allowed me to relate to these issues by living in what Yalom (1995) refers to as, "a state of mindfulness" (p. 94). That is, a state of being aware, living authentically and responsibly. It is my awareness of the capacity to be self-creative in the state of mindfulness that promotes the ability to change. I make art in order to live in a mindful way.

As I have worked with clients who are suffering from emotional and mental disturbances, I have come into intimate contact with people who have been physically, emotionally, or sexually abused. I have heard some incredibly painful and horrific stories during my career. I have seen countless images of shattered hearts, bleeding wrists, grim reapers, barren landscapes, defiled beds, invaded bodies, and broken promises. The weight of these images, and their accompanying stories, has been overwhelming at times. Seeing and hearing the effects of trauma, day in and day out, can become vicariously traumatic itself. Art therapists cannot avoid being moved by clients. We need not shield ourselves from our own powerful feelings. Yet, we cannot afford to be consistently overwhelmed and traumatized by our clients either. The most effective way for us to protect ourselves from vicarious traumatization is through making our own art. Making art provides a healthy, practical, and authentic mechanism for handling the intense feelings that accompany clinical work.

Art Making as a Form of Exploration and Documentation of Therapeutic Work

As art therapists, the truly unique gift we have to offer to the clinical milieu, whether it is a psychiatric hospital, physical rehabilitative hospital, public school, addictions recovery center, or geriatric nursing home, is our artistic sensibilities. Robbins (1988) writes, "The language of the artist and our psychoaesthetic perspective are our unique contribution to the treatment process" (p. 100). Making art is a *metaverbal* activity. The implication of this description is that it is beyond words. Aldridge (1993) comments, "it is important to emphasize that talking about therapy [or any activity] is always several steps removed" (p. 200).

Throughout much of our history, art therapists have worked in psychiatric treatment institutions and medical hospitals. In such institutions, the professionals whose disciplines have historically relied upon verbal interactions with the client have been held in the highest professional regard. In order for art therapists to be recognized as professional colleagues, and thereby assume some measure of influence and status within such institutions, it seemed necessary for them to incorporate, or assimilate, the language of the aforementioned disciplines. Hence, many art therapists absorbed the language of these disciplines and de-emphasized artistic or aesthetic descriptions of their work. Although this assimilation may have been necessary in the past, it may be important to consider reclaiming art making as a form of documentation.

How can artworks document therapeutic work? As I said earlier, painting, sculpting, and dancing are very different activities from *talking* about painting, sculpting, and dancing. Thus, there are times when it may be important to document our work as art therapists in metaverbal ways. As the old truism states, a picture is worth a thousand words. When I worked in a psychiatric hospital, I often took examples of client artworks to team meetings. Initially, I was shy about doing so, given that my colleagues on the team were all verbally oriented clinicians. I worried that the psychiatrist would overanalyze, or the psychologist would interpret, or the social worker would not really be interested in the client's artwork. More times than not, however, my teammates genuinely appreciated seeing the actual artworks rather than being limited to my verbal descriptions of them. By taking the images to the team meeting, I not only was able to honor the work of the client, but also was able to educate my fellow team members. This had the effect of enlivening and enriching team meetings.

In many instances, it is also important to take photographs of clients' artworks. Many art therapists do not have the facilities to store client work, and many others believe that artworks are the clients' property and should not be kept by the therapist. For these reasons, it may not be practical, or philosophically acceptable, to retain clients' actual art pieces. However, photographs and digital images can provide a lasting record of the artistic and therapeutic work that is truly beyond words. The important thing to remember is that the most poignant documentation of an art therapist's work may not be found in clinical notes, but rather in the images and artworks created in the therapeutic context.

Art Making as a Basis for Responsive Interaction with Clients

Making art in response to a particular person, or his or her artwork, is a potent way for the art therapist to engage in imaginal dialogue with the client-artist. I refer to this as an imaginative interpretive dialogue because the artist-therapist always projects her or his own feelings and thoughts into the artwork she or he creates in response to the client-artist. Typically, the client-artist is inspired to make another image in response to the therapist's response. This, in my view, is an incredibly valuable and authentic method of interpretive interaction that engages both parties in a process of deepening their relationship to one another.

I have offered an example of imaginative interpretive dialogue through relating the story of Bob, a man whom I saw in weekly art therapy sessions for nearly two years (Moon, 1997). Bob's psychiatrist asked me to consult with him because he was "stuck" in therapy. Bob complained that he never enjoyed anything. Although he was a successful and happily married man, he was melancholic.

His early images were rather tight and constricted renderings executed with a number two lead pencil. Although he was able to handle the pencil skillfully, he derived little or no gratification from his efforts and the finished products seemed devoid of emotional content. He routinely crumpled his drawings and threw them away at the end of the session.

I noticed that Bob's affect changed markedly whenever he talked about his teen years. Most of the time he was a rather rigid, guarded, and up-tight sort of person, but when he relayed stories of his adolescence, he would sometimes smile and visibly relax. At other times, he seemed to become indignant and angry as he talked about those years. In either case, it seemed that he livened up and became more expressive whenever he spoke of that time of his life.

It was my sense that the pencil drawing process was not helping Bob because he usually chose to discard the products of his work. This seemed to represent his desire to throw away parts, or all, of his life. So I decided to shift our work to painting.

One of the stories Bob told me had to do with the purchase of his first car, a VW Beetle. I could easily connect with that story because my first car was also a Beetle. As a first painting exercise, I had suggested that he try to do an abstract representation of the feelings he had during his adolescence. I decided to do a painting of the VW that Bob had described to me. Initially, I imagined it being on a tree-lined, circa 1950s, small town street. But somehow that did not seem right. During several sessions with Bob I painted over the street images and created a background that was a stereotypical plaza in front of a modern office complex. When the plaza background was finished, I envisioned the image of a man turning away from the Beetle.

During one particular session, as Bob painted at his easel, I was working on the image of the man turning away. Bob said, "You know, that guy reminds me of my dad."

I responded, "He is looking away from your car."

Bob replied, "Yeah, Dad never let himself have any fun."

"That is sad." I said.

Bob did not say anything but tears welled up in his eyes.

I made no effort to link his statement about his father to his own style of living his life, but he clearly was able to do so metaphorically. I did ask Bob what he thought I ought to title the painting. He suggested, "The Old Man Will Not Listen To His Past."

Responsive art making offers art therapists a way to encourage and work with multiple interpretations of clients' art. This is done by engaging with the client's art in an authentic manner, while avoiding the negative aspects of interpretation and labeling. The process of responsive art making brings the art therapist into a deeper understanding of the life of the client by intensifying empathy and providing another way of knowing the person. The process also serves as a basis for dialogue with the client-artist. Responsive art making is a form of interpretive dialogue with clients. It is anchored in a reverence for the mystery, the unverifiable qualities, of human existence and images. Robbins (1988) states, "As a therapeutic artist I carry the conviction that knowledge invariably transcends the limits of words."

Art Making as Spiritual Practice, or Participation in Soul Making

In *Working with Images: The Art of Art Therapists* (Moon, 2002), I solicited submissions of artworks and essays about art making from art therapists throughout North America. An independent jury committee selected 50 art therapists for inclusion in the text. It was intriguing to me to read their artists' statements. One especially interesting aspect was how many of the artists discussed their ideas regarding the relationship between art making and spiritual practice.

Hillman (1989) describes soul as a perspective that changes random events into meaningful happenings. I have long argued that such transformation is precisely what happens when one makes art. Making art is making soul. Art making creates a new perspective, an imaginative portrait of the artist. By painting, drawing, and sculpting, meanings are made visible as random events become ensouled experiences. The most profound gift of art therapists to clients and to clinical settings is the soul/art-making process.

Regardless of the form one's spirituality takes, whether Judaic, Christian, Zen, Islamic, or non-sectarian, it is inevitably reflected in, and expressed by, the things we create. As an art therapist, I view the work I do as a sacred journey that clients and I go on together. The mode of transportation is the doing of artistic work. Artworks become the outwardly visible parables and prayers that document the journey. In the shelter of our studios, soul is made in the midst of painted confessions, drawn thanksgivings, and sculpted praises. Thus, making art is a form of spiritual practice.

Art Making as the Basis of Authentic Relationship with Self and Others

The image of the canvas mirror provides an apt metaphor for the introspective process that is one of the cornerstones of art making (Moon 1990, 1995). There have been times when I have looked into the mirror and found images of beauty, valor, and honesty. At other times, I have seen open blisters, images of isolation, and fearfulness. It all depends upon what is going on in my life. Sometimes I have tried to look away from these canvas mirror images, but this seems only to accentuate their power. There is no getting away from the pleasure and pain of artistic inquiry into the self.

As I have considered the prerequisite of artistic activity for art therapists, the metaphoric image of the canvas mirror has emerged again. It is necessary for art therapists to continually strive for self-awareness. It is impossible to have an authentic relationship with another person if you are out of touch with yourself. Self-awareness is stimulated through artistic self-reflection and self-transparency.

An important by-product of self-awareness for art therapists is the capacity to weave together their identities as professional therapists, artists, and human beings in the context of art therapy relationships. Art therapists ask clients to engage in art making as a means of clarifying and expressing identity. Clients are encouraged to look at artistic creations as autonomous entities that suggest potential meanings and lead to recognizing different options in life. For the therapist who guides clients in such explorations through art, it is important to practice what he or she preaches. In order to establish authentic relationships with clients, it is vital that art therapists make art.

In my experience, clients often benefit from the commitment and enthusiasm of the artist-therapist. This enthusiasm is most visible in the art therapist's own artistic work. When an art therapist is actively engaged in her own expressive art tasks, a positive sense of contagion is created that is powerful medicine. Creating this sense of artistic contagion is absolutely dependent upon the therapist. One cannot expect clients to be able to generate artistic exuberance of their own accord. Clients who are in need of therapy often do not feel positively about themselves, and therefore often are not enthusiastic about much of anything. On the contrary, the people who most often are referred to art therapy are typically suffering, or angry, or hurt individuals, so the generation of artistic infectiousness is the therapist's responsibility.

A colleague once remarked that looking at others' artworks often left him feeling as if he'd been invited into a confessional cell. I think this describes my thoughts about making art. As I create, there is a sense of intimacy and immediacy that detaches me from intellectual objectivity. This detachment paradoxically allows me to enter into my own depths. Paintings have the capacity to become our confessions, portraits of how we see the world around us, how we see our place in the world, and how the world is expressed within us.

As an artist therapist, I believe in the power and the goodness of art making. Again, Allen (1992) writes, "The most crucial factor in the life or death of the field of art therapy is not certification, not licensure, but whether sufficient numbers of individual art therapists maintain an ongoing connection to their own art" (p. 28). The most difficult periods of my professional life have been those when, for one reason or another, I have been inactive artistically. In those times, my work gave me little pleasure. Berry (1990) writes, "More and more, we assume that if we want to be pleased we must wait until evening, or the weekend, or vacation, or retirement . . . We are defeated at work because our work gives us no pleasure" (pp. 139–140). It is in the studio that my work life is in sync with my soul, and it is from that place of soul that my identity as an artist therapist is nurtured.

As I work in my painting studio, I try to foster a sense of awe and commitment to the notion that the image can, and should, just be. I am not proposing an anti-verbal doctrine; rather, I am working toward a pro-meta-verbal faith in image metaphors. If paint is in the veins of this artist-therapist, metaphor is in my heart. As I make art, I contend with the notion that the things I create are partial self-portraits. The images that come through me are both themselves and a description their creator.

In the art studio, drawings and paintings provide snapshots of inner life. Every line, every color, and every shape are pieces of realities that resist verbal description. The arts offer an authentic communication mode that is often lacking in other aspects of life.

As I paint, I am intensely aware of my relationship to the processes, materials, and images that surface. With each brush stroke, the client tells her tale, as I do. Together we set the stage for the sharing of stories that is the basis of the art therapy pilgrimage. As I open myself to understanding what has been expressed, I establish a safe milieu in which client-artists may engage in their own self-explorations. We make art in order to communicate. Such authentic communication would not be possible if I refrained from making art.

The process of creating art is a metaphor for life itself in that as the artist works, she has ultimate power to change the piece. She can change the lines, brighten or darken color, add shadows or highlights. The painter can, if she chooses, paint over the piece and start again. This is a parable of life itself. It can be changed, if and when the individual decides to change. Many times the client does not believe she has such power over the path of her own life. Making art becomes an introduction to free will and the power of selection and creating. Creating empowers.

Why should art therapists make art?

We make art in order to clarify, express, and contain our feelings that surface in therapeutic work. We make art in order to explore and document our therapeutic work. We make art in order to responsively interact with clients. We make art in order to engage in a kind of spiritual practice and to participate in soul-making. Finally, we make art in order to form authentic relationships with others and with ourselves.

Chapter III

BEGINNINGS

The Third Essential–Becoming an art therapist is not easy.

THE STORY OF IT
(A FAIRY TALE)

In a land known as Wo, there lived a girl of 14 summers. She was a kind and gentle girl, not beautiful, but not unattractive either. However, she was troubled. A question had arisen within her during the summer of her twelfth year: *What is the meaning of It?* Although she tried to put it out of her mind, the question would not go away. Every day, hundreds of times, she found herself wondering, *What does It mean?*

Oh, she knew people said *it is too bad.* Her mother, in an angry mood one day, said, "It is your father's fault." Her older brother told her *it bugged him.* Sometimes she overheard her aunts and uncles muttering that *she would never make it.* The only thing she didn't know was what *it* meant. The question haunted her day and night. Sometimes she would dream that she was opening a large box where *it* would be, but she always woke up too soon to see it.

During the summer of her fourteenth year, she was so vexed by it that she decided at last she must do something. She decided to run away. She intended to ask everyone she met what was the meaning of *it.*

Finally, on the morning of the middle day of the middle month of the season, she crept out of her house and began her journey. Everywhere she went she asked the people she met what *It* meant. A constable told her it was the law. An athlete told her it was winning. A businessman told her it was profit, and two lovers told her it was just being together.

While all these answers seemed plausible enough, somehow for her, they just didn't seem quite right. And so she traveled and asked, walked and listened, but was never satisfied. At long last, worn out and feeling defeated, she decided to return home. That night as she slept, she had a dream.

In the dream, she walked across a desert and was very, very thirsty. She came upon a shimmering lake. She knelt down on the bank and tried to scoop some water with one hand. She had to be cautious, for she could not swim and she wasn't sure of the depth of the water. The wanderer was so thirsty, but each time she tried to scoop water with her hand, it all ran out of her grasp before she could get it to her lips. In the dream, she felt that she might die if she couldn't quench her thirst.

Suddenly an old woman appeared on the bank beside her. The old woman had long silvery hair and was dressed in a blue cloak. She reached out and gently touched the girl's shoulder. "You must use both hands," she said.

The girl shuddered, "But I might fall in and drown!"

The old woman sat quietly for a bit, then said, "You may die of thirst or die of drowning. I tell you, you must decide to risk."

The girl's throat was parched and she longed for the cool relief. "Couldn't you help me?"

The old woman frowned, then gently sighed, "I am not thirsty. You must decide. That is all there is to it." With that, she disappeared.

* * *

Becoming an art therapist is not easy. Students come to training seeking the meaning of *It* for their lives. With them they bring all the answers they have been given throughout their history. They bring volumes of questions, mental cassette tapes full of self-definitions and catalogues of how they think the world should be. The mentors' tasks are to help students question their answers, answer their questions; edit, delete, and re-record their self-definitions; and expand their repertoire of ideas, feelings, and values in relation to their experience of the world.

JOURNEY

Sometime in the middle of August, 1985, I was in my classroom at the Columbus College of Art and Design, where I was teaching undergraduate art therapy courses. The college hosted an annual open house at which faculty members from all the various divisions gave presentations or led discussions about their specialty areas. On that particular evening, I was surprised by the appearance in my room of Mary Lou Powers. I had known Lou for several years. At that time she was a teacher specializing in educating severely learning handicapped children and adolescents in the on-campus school at Harding Hospital.

Our paths had crossed professionally from time to time, but we had not gotten along very well. My impression of Lou was that she was rather hostile and liked to be in charge. She seemed to challenge other staff in a devaluing way. Lou recalls that she initially perceived me to be overly competitive, flamboyant, and controlling. In short, neither of us cared much for the other. Therefore I was somewhat uneasy when, after hearing my presentation about art therapy, Lou informed me that she intended to register for one of my classes.

I worried about how she would fit in with a class of college sophomores and juniors. Lou already had nearly 20 years of teaching experience. Obviously, she would be at a very different level than her fellow students. I also worried that she might be difficult to deal with in class. I had heard from colleagues at the hospital of her reputation for assertive critical engagement in meetings. I wondered if I was competent to teach a woman like Lou.

The semester began three weeks after the open house. True to her word, Lou had signed up for the class. She sat in the front row. There was no escape; I had to establish a relationship with her. We began.

My first lecture to new groups of students begins, "All things we create are a partial self-portrait." In my ruminations on my fears about Lou's participation in the class, I had failed to have faith in the awesome power of art processes. In the 32 weeks (two semesters) that followed, Lou painted and drew and scribbled portraits of herself as I had never imagined her. Perhaps most poignant was a drawing in which she depicted herself as having an outer layer of rhinoceros hide concealing and protecting her real, inner doeskin. Images of a broken marriage, a troubled son, an ill brother, and a vulnerable self emerged. Our relationship transformed from a dance reminiscent of heavyweight boxers circling and measuring one another, to a rather awkward ballet. In the midst of our unfolding relationship, Lou began to ask questions about the Harding Graduate Clinical Art Therapy Program that I co-directed. Near the end of her second semester, she applied for admission to the program and was accepted for entry the following fall.

The initial educational plan designed for Lou focused on four primary components.

First, since Lou came to the program with vast experience as a teacher with adolescents, we agreed to provide her with clinical art therapy exposure to the adult clients at the hospital. Her original schedule included an exercise group, horticulture therapy, an adult expressive arts group, and creative arts studio. She was also assigned to work with a psychiatric team on the long-term adult unit.

Second, the faculty was concerned that Lou's engagement with and knowledge of visual arts media was deficient. In order to address this, she was urged to explore a variety of fine arts modalities in the creative arts studio. Among these were painting, drawing, and sculpture.

Third, Lou was registered into the Philosophy of Art Therapy Seminar and the Group Process in Art Therapy seminar. The focus was to be the development of a personal philosophy of treatment, with opportunities for experimental implementation and integration of academic, clinical, and artistic experiences.

Finally, she was assigned an individual art therapy supervisor/mentor who would serve as her guide through the graduate educational process.

A cornerstone of the mentor-student relationship was the student's journal (Fig. 5). The journal was to be written on a daily basis and was to reflect the journey of the student through the training process. The journal was often a sketchbook as well, chronicling in pictures the intensity of the educational experience. The students were given very few guidelines for the journal. All they were told was that it was to be kept current and that it would be viewed by the mentor/supervisor on a weekly basis.

To help the reader understand the early stages of the art therapy educational journey, the following excerpts from Lou's journal are offered. Names of clients and student peers have been changed for purposes of protecting confidentiality.

Figure 5. The journal was often a sketchbook chronicling in pictures the intensity of the educational experience.

6/20 Bruce asks
      But why do we do art?
      I don't understand "soul."
      Art proclaims, I AM, I AM.
      What about the dignity of man?

6/21 —stretch—
      Pull gently.
      Bandana Lady!
      "Can I love you?"
      You don't scare me!
      I've seen your pain.
      Relationship. . . .
      Relationship. . . .
      Relationship. . . .

Relationship. . . .
Process . . . Climb the mountain

6/23 A whole week here. I love it.
No fussing about being therapeutic.
Imagine.

INTERN PROCESS GROUP:
Young, your scab.
All nervous, excited.
It's out there.
Mysterious Dana
Who says one thing but secrets another
And dear Josh.
Caren, I'm glad you are here!

Completed flower drawing. It's good.
Adults are just adolescents in grown-up bodies.
The tasks are the same!

6/24 Dear Bruce,
Why do I do art?
Because you say, do art.
Once long ago I did art
Because I had to, perhaps I'll rediscover that person.
  One thing is for sure
  I do therapy because I have to, it swells
  inside and bubbles out.

ARPS HALL
  A visit to the library reaffirms my quest.
  I know that if I don't continue to learn and study and grow,
  I'll go stagnant.

6/26 I feel more in the flow
  I gave Laurie a tour of the school—
  So much of my ego still there.
  Wanted to join Ruth, Ali and Gail today
  Perhaps adults are important too—

I always thought kids were the main focus of my energies.
Oh, Barri! So young, so full of life—
What joy to share this time with you.
How short the time is.
A pressing need to know all.
Where will this lead?

6/28 Working with the adjunctive therapy staff is a real treat.
I experience none of the crazy hostile feeling. Why?
Truly a nurturing staff. I'm able to let the doeskin show.
We had lunch at a Chinese place.
Wonderful—I'm reconnecting with Andy, it's been years.
Jane shared her eating disorder with me.
I shared my L.D. problems in group with her.
My name tag says Lou Powers, A.T.

6/29 I'm painfully aware of how short my time is.
My worst fantasy has come true, I love this.
Why do I do art?
Because Bruce says, "Draw,"
and I can find parts of my youth in the task.
I experience total absorption,
but will I continue to draw? Who knows?
Why do therapy? Because I can't not do therapy.
It flows from within, not to do it is to die.

PROCESS GROUP:
Deb asked again if I was protecting Josh.
I hope not, the pain will be suffered.
Perhaps it's my effort to join his journey.
If he won't come to us, admit membership,
Then I'll go to him.
Dana—finally her affect fit her voice.
I struggle to include Jan, but am certainly aware that she is an
outsider. The experience is not the same for her.
Caren continues to look brighter, more confident in herself.
I hope I shared the pain of David,
the years of doubt.

7/4 Perhaps I'm finding the artist in me. It was there at one time,
adolescence. Cathy Moon's suggestion that I selected art
   therapy for a
reason must be true. Thank you.
My research in sexual abuse confirms what I've been seeing
   in the
adolescent population here. More abused kids, both male and
   female.
Generational abuse and relationship between abuse and self-
mutilation.

7/5 I was very anxious in research group.
Probably because of Caren. My topic, sexual abuse, is a good
   one
considering the number of patients we serve with this problem,
   but my
knowledge of her abuse made it harder.
I don't want to leak this information to the group members,
   but let
Caren tell it in her own time.
I was angry when Deb pushed her. Countertransference issues
may remind me of my own passivity?
Perhaps, what willing victims we all were–(women)
I was upset that my art might be uninteresting.
The artist is alive.

7/7 Judy and I had a terrific expressive art group. We seem to work so
well together. An extra pair of ears and eyes.
What a nice flow. I really respect her and feel that she respects me
too. We have shared issues and concerns. This feels right.
What about relationship is so scary?
She talked about controlling relationship
Ending when she can't be in charge.
How can someone love me after all that I've been through.
If I pull the bandage off to make myself vulnerable, I risk losing a
friend–it's painful, especially if I value friendship more than
they do.

PROCESS GROUP:
Some in the group see Bruce and Deb as authority figures.
Josh continues to distance himself
Caren and I had a mini after-group discussion, just comforting
    and
acknowledging Josh's pain and our support of him.

7/13 I must put limits on Diane. She is very devaluing.
      How hard this seems to be compared to adolescents.
      I've set limits with her before, so I will again.
      I need to explore fantasy in expressive arts group.
      I want to let patients know my world.
      So many questions about Josh.
      Obviously he is very frightened of intimacy.
      I just want his friendship, not his body.
      I guess I'll never know.
      Bruce—I bought two blank canvases.
      What about that?

7/19 I've been neglectful of this journal process.
      I started painting today. It felt good mixing colors,
      putting brush to canvas.
      in my mind's eye I have an image,
      perhaps my hand will create this.
      Jody, Caren and I chatted after work about art, technique,
      process—
      I actually sounded like I knew what I was talking about.
      Well, reading is my strong point.
      We will see if my hand can make what my eye has read.
      I have never experienced such acceptance and validation of self-
      worth as I have this summer.
      Even staff members whom I don't work with have made positive
      comments.

7/25 Big thrill, but scary.
      Jody wants me to lead her expressive arts group while she's on
      vacation. I'm on my own.
      I feel more confident, stronger.
      How good it is to be valued.

7/27 POEM
> My object is saddened, confused and empathic.
> A sudden breeze
> will it spin . . . or fall.
> Two pieces, yet one
> each unto itself.
> My journey has begun.
> The risk must be taken.
> From some protective mother's,
> brother's, lover's, father's arm.
> On to wilderness, to change.
> Softness returns as red,
> raw violence abates.
> From pain and conflict to life and growth.
>
> Lou Powers

In this slice of life, this quick glimpse of two months of Lou's inner commentary on her training to become an art therapist, we catch the shiny surfaces and difficult shadows of her experience. A recurring reference throughout Lou's journal is to my questioning her, "Why do you make art?" It reflects the major thrust of her experience in training. It is important to remember that Lou came to the program after nearly 20 years' experience in teaching learning disabled adolescents in a psychiatric setting. For her, there was little or no question of her academic background or clinical/relationship skills. What Lou clearly lacked was (1) an understanding of the visual arts language, and (2) a view of herself as an artist/therapist. For Lou's professional and personal growth, it was essential that she engage in a training program capable of flexing to meet her particular educational needs.

"Learning art therapy demands a good deal of openness and self-confrontation. For many, this mode of learning is alien to their entire style of privacy and control (Robbins & Sibley, 1976, p. 11). Robbins and Sibley identify two prominent problematic areas for art therapy students, " (1) issues relating to the development of a professional role; and (2) the particular strengths and vulnerabilities an artist brings to a training program" (p. 13). Becoming an art therapist involves the development of one's own therapeutic style. This is a process as individual as one's own art products. This is not an easy process.

Chapter IV

BEGINNER'S CHAOS

The Fourth Essential–From chaos comes order.

Although students come to art therapy education with varied academic and personal histories, it is relatively safe to assume that the early stages of their educational journey are experienced as chaotic. In graduate art therapy programs, some students are admitted who are fresh from undergraduate school while others may already hold an advanced degree in a related field. Some students may be as young as 21 years old, while others may be middle-aged or beyond. Some have had extensive experience with psychological treatment; others have had little or no contact with the emotionally disturbed. Regardless of students' backgrounds, one commonality is that beginning graduate school is often a chaotic experience. As educators, we are behooved to remain aware of the disorientation that new environments, new expectations, and new experiences can create (Fig. 6).

While every graduate art therapy program has its own idiosyncrasies, there are general factors that lead to beginner's chaos. Among these factors are the realities of finding one's way around a new campus and/or practicum facility. This often requires learning the names of unfamiliar buildings and their location on an unknown campus. There are specific rooms and areas within each of these buildings with which the art therapy student must become familiar. Some areas of clinical settings may be open to public access while other areas may be restricted. Along with the geographical layout of the campus and clinical site, students are quickly introduced to a host of new people. They begin their relationships with program administrators, faculty members, supervisors, peers, adjunct personnel, and clients. In clinical settings, students are also quickly engaged in meetings where they may interact with a host of other professionals: doctors, social workers, nurses, medical directors, psychologists, teachers, aids, techni-

Figure 6. The early stages of the journey are chaotic.

cians, and more. In the first week of graduate school, the student may easily encounter 50 or more new people. This in itself can be overwhelming.

Another aspect of the chaos is that beginning graduate school marks the end of anticipating and planning for future education. Most students have thought long and hard about their choice of careers. Many students have had to make sacrifices in order to be in graduate school. Some have waited a long time between their initial decision to enter graduate school and actually beginning the process. These circumstances lead to internal anxiety as the training is begun.

Students also often struggle with their own doubts as they embark on this new phase of their lives. They are plagued by questions such as: *Is this what I really want to do? Do they like me? Am I really good enough to be successful here? What if I don't like it here after I've started?* Many old feelings of insecurity may be stirred as the training starts.

Finally, add to this mix the mysterious nature of the creative arts therapy field itself and we begin to glimpse the new students' internal experiences as they take the first steps of their journey. It is as if their world were one of those glass balls with white flakes suspended in liquid. Entry into graduate education to become an arts therapist is a little like shaking the glass, creating a snowstorm. Yet, in many instances the flurry remains hidden and internal while the student's exterior appears smooth and undisturbed. Certainly no graduate student in any field wants to be seen as in turmoil. It is the responsibility of the faculty supervisor to be *tuned in* to the experience of the student.

The initial chaos of the student is ultimately necessary and of great benefit. It is necessary in that entry into graduate school is a fairly dramatic transitional period in the student's life. An old way of being is left behind while a new way is as yet unclear. As are all passages in life, this is accompanied with a measure of fear, excitement, and anxiety. These feelings are of benefit to the student in that they present her or him with a potent, double-edged theme that should become a powerful tool in both educational pursuits and in professional practice down the road.

On one edge of this "beginner's chaos" theme is the art process itself. The sensitive educator will engage the student in this metaphor by discussing the parallels of beginning graduate school and starting a new art work. As the artist approaches the studio, the possibilities are endless (Fig. 7). Countless subtle choices are made consciously and unconsciously. What medium will be used? In the case of a painting, what size and shape of canvas? What tools will be employed? Will the painting be representational or non-representational? Abstract or highly rendered? Content? Color? Form? Shape? Emotional tone? . . . and on and on. There are thousands, even millions of potential images that could emerge as the artist works. These choices make up the chaotic sea of possibilities. Each question the artist answers, each decision made as the work unfolds serves to bring structure and order to the chaos so the artistic process and product can be realized. Perhaps the deepest sense of gratification and connection to our work that we artists can experience comes from this profound process of making order from disordered potential.

It is through the multiple decisions, subtle and overt, that the artist begins to uncover the essence of an art piece. The artist may never put this essential quality into words, yet it is comprehended at a deep level that is either pre- or meta-verbal.

The engagement in art processes is an enactment of one's potential to structure the chaos of multiple possibilities. This is exactly the same position in which the new trainees find themselves. The possibilities are numerous and at first seem confusing and jumbled. Some of their internal questions are, *Is this field valid? How will this profession help me to blend my love of art with my desire to be a therapist? What is the most important—process or product? What kinds of clients do I want to work with? What will I do well? What if I do harm to someone? Why do I want to do this work?*

It is important, in all stages of graduate training but particularly in the initial phases, to frequently refer the student to the art process itself. I have vivid recall of a student coming into my office for a supervisory session and slamming my door. She sat down and immediately poured out the anger she felt toward a psychiatrist who had made an offhand, devaluing comment about art therapy. He had referred to a group of which my student was a co-leader as "voodoo group." I knew the psychiatrist was intending to make a joke, but his attempt at humor had pushed my student's buttons. I let her vent for a few minutes, and then shifted the conversation towards a more detached observing-ego position. I suggested that we explore all the possible interpretations we could make of the psychiatrist's "voodoo" comment.

The student's anger rapidly dissolved into tears as she got in touch with her own feelings of inadequacy and doubts about the art therapy profession. Questions came so quickly, with no time for attempts at answers, that my supervisory role became that of an empathic listener. As the session neared its close, there was still much to be addressed. I suggested that she spend some time in the studio making art.

The next morning I found three vivid drawings lying on a chair in my office (Fig. 8).

The images were intense. The first was a tangled mass of color and line, reminiscent of a large pile of knotted yarn scraps. The second image utilized the same colors, but there was a vague hint of a facial form in the turmoil of lines. The third image was a self-portrait. The colors were consistent with those of the first two drawings and, although there were still knots and tangles in the lines, the face was clearly represented. In an artistic sense, the student had laid out the road map of her internal journey. These three drawings became our starting point for many supervisory sessions. What began as a jumbled, angry, hurt mass of colorful lines eventually formed a coherent self-portrait. By the time her clinical rotation at that practicum site ended, she was able to joke with the psychiatrist about the *voodoo* she does and the *art* of medicine that he practiced.

The other edge of the beginner's chaos theme relates to the parallel between embarking on the educational journey and the client's experience in beginning treatment. The confusion, pain, anxiety, excitement and fears generated in the student are a wonderful resource, for they connect the art therapy student with the client's experience.

The longer an arts therapist practices, the harder it is to stay attuned to the internal turmoil of the client. Doing art therapy becomes what is normal and routine for the art therapist. The awe and newness inevitably diminishes as the therapist becomes more seasoned. It is important to impress upon the student how similar are his or her fears, hopes, and anxieties in beginning training to those of the client entering treatment. These feelings are a precious window into the world of the client.

Figure 7. As the artist approaches the studio the possibilities are endless.

Figure 8. What began as a jumbled, angry, hurt mass of colorful lines eventually formed a coherent self-portrait.

Chapter V

THE JOURNEY METAPHOR IN EDUCATION

The Fifth Essential–Becoming an
art therapist is a difficult journey.

The hero or heroine, whether of fairy tale, myth or movie, often begins the transformation from ordinary life to heroic life by embarking upon a journey. The quest is marked by encounters with forces of evil and good. It has pitfalls and terrible moments when the heroine fears that her efforts have been folly and all is lost. The journey is sometimes a descent into the darkness of the soul, where the engagements with powerful forces are not of the external sort, but rather are the internal wrestlings of virtue and the vile. Ultimately, the hero comes to terms with both the forces of his inner life and the powers of the world. Whether by killing or taming or naming them, the hero emerges from the struggle forever changed (Fig. 9).

As I sit in my office at the college interviewing prospective students, I often think of the image of the heroine. I try to tell applicants for graduate school what a difficult and treacherous journey they are volunteering for. I mention the constant stream of books and articles to be read, the papers to be researched and written. I speak of the stress of spending hours a day in clinical settings that are often tense, painful, and exhausting. I tell stories about clients I have known, about their battered pasts, their abused childhoods, their shattered present and bleak future. I warn these would-be heroes of the strenuous physical schedule they will be expected to follow. And I tell them of the emotional calluses I've had to grow.

After all that, I talk about the joy of seeing a client leave therapy who has really made the sought-for gains. I speak of love and tenderness, spirit and art.

Some prospective students come to me as they are nearing the end of undergraduate careers in the fine arts, psychology, or art education.

Figure 9. The quest is marked by encounters with agents of evil and good.

Others are middle-aged, restless with their current professions and vaguely unhappy with the course their lives have taken. Their children are now in school. They feel called to a different life. Still another group of would-be therapists already possess advanced degrees from related disciplines. They long for a creative educational experience. Regardless of their age, background, or motivations, I try to frame with them the concept of the heroic journey engendered by training to become an art therapist.

The tightly intertwined phenomena of art, therapy, and personal heroic quest form the foundation of the field. These processes swirl together and force tremendous demands upon the student. The individual is called to new levels of emotional, physical, cognitive, and spiritual involvement in the struggle to become an art therapist. The intensity of the journey led one of our recent interns, Darienne Veri, to exclaim, "It's not a normal life!" I could only agree that being an art therapist is not a normal life, and surely being in the early stages of becoming one accentuates the abnormality. One must be ready and willing to go on a heroic journey.

Students often begin their quest with excitement and enthusiasm, not unlike the honeymoon and newlywed periods of marriage. It is fun. Everything is new and interesting. They are filled with energy. Very soon, however, their excitement is tempered by the powerful realities of clients in extreme emotional pain, with brutal histories and tragic experiences in the present. Enthusiasm is transformed into self-doubt, dismay, and confusion. Inevitably the student's comfortable self-image is challenged by deep intrapsychic stirrings.

Becoming an art therapist requires an extraordinary willingness to introspect and struggle with the images one finds in the mirror. It is often quite difficult. The student who comes from a fine arts background at times sees the personal exploration and self-confrontation as intrusive and threatening to expressive freedom. With these students, the recurrent question, "Why do you make art?" may be heard as an impingement on their creativity. Such a student lamented, "Why do I need to know? Isn't it enough that I *do* make art?"

To some students, the making of self as the subject of inquiry may seem foreign. These students begin with the belief that all they need to know about a given subject must be written somewhere in the literature of the field. For them, the first few steps of their heroic quest are filled with reluctance and concern. All novice art therapists must wrestle with a new mode of learning in which they are both subject and object of inquiry.

A STORY

In a certain tribe of nomads, it was the custom to send scouts into the desert to find water. For some time now, the scouts had been disappearing, and the chief was growing concerned. The tribe was beginning to question his wisdom in sending the men out. Yet the chief knew that they must seek water. He began to send the scouts out two by two. They vanished. The next scouts went in parties of five. They too disappeared without a trace. The situation was becoming critical, but the chief did not know what to do.

At about that time, a young would-be heroine arrived at the tent village. She sought out the chief and told him she'd heard they were having some trouble. The chief explained the situation, adding that he was feeling quite desperate. "Don't worry," said the young woman, "I will go out into the desert for you, and I will find water."

The would-be heroine left the village and struck out into the barren wilderness. When she reached a certain place, she found a large crack in the earth. A cold wind surged up from the darkness. For a moment the heroine hesitated, then asked herself, "What in the world am I getting myself into? Why should I care if that tribe back there has water? This looks like a dangerous place" (Fig. 10).

As doubts echoed within her, she began to back away from the crevice. The crack lengthened and followed her. The farther she withdrew, the closer came the cold darkness. She realized that if she turned and ran, she would be swallowed up. She stood paralyzed for several moments. Suddenly the wind gusted and sand swirled about her. A hooded figure appeared, shimmering in the blowing sand. He spoke.

"You must not run away from this place."

The heroine replied, "But this is more than I bargained for. What can I do?"

Again the hooded figure spoke, "You must not run away, and you cannot stay where you are. The dilemma is your own." With that, the figure disappeared into the sand.

The would-be heroine did the only thing she could. She turned to face the darkness and slowly walked down through the opening. There she discovered a hidden river. On the far bank she saw the remains of the tribal scouts who had preceded her, who had tried to run from the darkness.

* * *

The process of becoming an art therapist continually challenges the defenses of the novice. There is a steady focus on the hidden underground rivers of the student's life and of the lives of clients she comes into contact with. For many students, this is a period of unprecedented growth.

In many ways, the success or failure of the journey depends upon the quality of the relationships among the student, faculty, and the mentor/supervisor. While it is clearly the work of the student that determines the ultimate outcome of the educational experience, these relationships fuel, guide, correct, and console the apprentice in mid-journey.

Figure 10. This looks like a dangerous place.

Chapter VI

THE MENTOR SUPERVISOR

The Sixth Essential–The success of art therapy education weighs heavily upon the shoulders of the mentor.

I believe that one of the vital elements of an effective art therapy educational experience is the relationship between a student and her mentor/supervisor. Supervision is defined as, "the direction and critical evaluation of instruction" (Webster, 1988). The word is derived from the Latin *super* (over) and *videre* (to watch, to see). Therefore, a supervisor is an overseer, one who watches over the work of another with responsibility for its quality.

This definition emphasizes the administrative functions of supervision, such as seeing to it that tasks are executed at acceptable quantitative and qualitative levels. As the director of a graduate art therapy education program, I must sometimes confront issues related to work: faculty load, class schedules, tardiness, or expectations in the workplace. However, this type of administrative supervision is seldom used in my relationship with students in the educational milieu.

A second aspect of supervision is the provision of education for the supervisee. Here the relationship is defined as a cooperative process through which the supervisor helps the supervisee use the educational structure to gain the best possible learning experience. It is this function of supervision that is most often the focus of the relationship between student and instructor. This aspect of supervision also responds to the student's desire for a relationship with someone who knows the answers.

While the first definition emphasizes the functional objectives of the educational setting (administrative), the second emphasizes the cognitive development of the student (educational). Each of these is only a partial description of supervision responsibilities. It is true that creative arts therapy supervision is both an administrative and educational process. The experienced art therapy practitioner has responsibility for implementing both functions in working with students, but there is more.

There is yet another markedly different responsibility that must be included in any definition of art therapy supervision. This is the supportive, expressive role-modeling function of supervision. The supervisor has the responsibility to maintain student morale, to help with the inevitable discouragements and doubts that arise and to model a quality of professionalism that will foster a sense of worth for the novice. In this way the art therapy supervisor remains in contact with his or her own dual inner images of self as a creator of art objects and as the artist of self-transformation.

These three primary aspects of supervision are complementary. When each is attended to properly, we begin to approach the *Mentor* model of supervision. The mentor model of supervision requires the establishment of an enlightened and supportive relationship in which the mentor is clearly identified as the master of the discipline. The mentor is dedicated to transferring her wealth of experience and knowledge to the student. In the tradition of acceptable paradox, the mentor is above the novice in a hierarchical system, yet deeply committed to the process of the heroic journey, on which she is a fellow pilgrim. Thus the mentor is a deep resource of technical information, a participant in an institutional political system, a capable container for swirling emotional currents and a willing companion who will honor the quest of the student (Fig. 11).

In this age of specialization and boundary definition, the mentor traverses the blurred lines between education and therapy. The art therapy student inevitably will struggle with his or her own developmental and psychological issues that are stirred by contact with patients. The mentor's response is to gently raise the mirror and ask, "What do you see?" Learning to be an art therapist is not an exercise in memorization. There are no formulas that say, *when the client does this, you must do that.*

Each new student presents unique challenges to the mentor. One student may view the mentor as an unnecessary burden, an authority who must be manipulated and avoided whenever possible. Another student may seize the opportunity for emotional support and subtly seeks personal therapy under the guise of instruction. Another student may project unresolved parental conflicts onto the relationship, setting

Figure 11. The mentor asks, "What do you see?"

up a battleground in the early stages of the educational journey. Some students see the mentor as invulnerable. Some see issues of control. Some seek protection while others long to compete. The attitude that the intern brings to the relationship has deep personal meaning.

These are the starting places for supervisor and supervisee, much like the initial transferences the client brings to therapy. The mentor begins the journey by honoring the student's early feelings, in the belief that they are the first road markers. The mentor is attentive to these early feelings, for they give direction as to how the journey should proceed. It is the mentor's task to see the student clearly and to approach the student/mentor relationship humbly and with reverence. It is, after all, the student who is embarking on the heroic quest; the mentor has been this way before. The mentor does not allow any initial counterfeelings toward the student to get in the way, but is still and attending. While it is the student who will do most of the work, success cannot be attained without a deep and honest relationship with a supervisor.

On the students' first day in Harding Hospital program I would ask each one to begin keeping a journal. I asked them to write or draw in it every day. They are to record their impressions of faculty members, peers, clients, therapists, how they feel about being in the program, et cetera. I inform them that I will read their journals once a week, before our regularly scheduled supervisory sessions.

The journal entries of students in the first few weeks of training often bear resemblances to one another. Some questions recur:

Why am I here?

Is this what I really want to do?

How will I ever be able to understand all this?

What is art therapy? Is it valid?

Listen to an entry from the journal of Joan Selle:

9/12/89

Yesterday, my first day, was in some ways exciting and in other ways overwhelming. I realize how much I have to learn. By the time I arrived home yesterday I felt kind of numb. I had been bombarded by so many emotions, I hardly felt anything. Just numbness.

Whether the student begins with a sense of overwhelmed numbness, or with rigidly set answers to the questions listed above, it quickly becomes evident to them that there are no precise paths to follow.

The mentor patiently suggests to both the lost and the falsely secure that there are no cookbook definitions or ready-made roles that will be enough for their journey.

In the middle of one supervisory session, a student sat sobbing. A colleague had given her some critical feedback regarding her style of dress. He said it was seductive. She exclaimed, "I can't help looking the way I do. Damn it, Bruce, tell me what to do!"

I sat quietly and she continued. "If you would just give me a rule book. First I mess up in the expressive art group by not saying enough. Then I talked to a client in the studio that I wasn't supposed to. Now *he* says I am too seductive. I give up!"

I responded by telling her about Franz Kafka's (1930) character K., who so desperately wants to gain entry into The Castle. K., I tell her, is anguished by the conflicting instructions he receives from the authorities of The Castle. "You remind me of K.," I tell her. "You so long for someone to tell you how to go about this training program. I'm sorry, I can give you some ideas and guidelines, but I can't tell you exactly how to become an art therapist. Some things you just have to learn through trial and error. But I will certainly go through this process with you."

Gradually the student abandons the search for easy answers and clear formulas. Some students celebrate their newfound freedom to learn. Others cling stubbornly to the style of education that has become familiar to them during the first 16 years of formal study. The transforming power of the art process eventually asserts itself and a phenomenological art therapy approach to art therapy education emerges. As this metamorphosis occurs, there is a coinciding decrease in the student's interest in simplistic theories, coupled with the student's increased awareness of the existential issues faced by clients. These changes do not happen easily. They often force an unprecedented level of anguish and introspection. At this point, the mentor must be willing to hold the pain of the apprentice.

As the students struggle to let go of the wish for an easy way through the educational process, many seek personal therapy. I see this as a strength in the novice, the ability to search out the medicine he or she is prescribing to others. At such times, the training process becomes the acceptable paradox: supporting the student as both healer and seeker of healing. This is a crucial experience for all involved, for it forces a new level of maturity upon students. They can no longer artificially separate themselves from their clients by saying, "I am here to serve you." Likewise, it thrusts upon the mentor memories of the first steps on her own journey, when she was not the master, but rather the frightened pilgrim. The student is reminded of the common humanity of the mentor, the client, and herself. The mentor is reminded of shared experience with both client and pupil. The client may also feel a new sense of safety with the novice therapist.

The student is placed in an exquisite position for learning. He must maintain a professional demeanor with clients, even while exploring the emotional rivers within himself. Questions arise about personal integrity and honesty. How can I be of help to this client when I feel so much turmoil myself? What good am I when I feel the same thing the client does? Shouldn't I tell clients the truth about my feelings that are similar to theirs?

Again, a passage from a student's journal:

> Staying safe versus facing fear. I'm not sure whether this is an option for me. Sometimes I choose safety, other times I risk. I need both. It takes sensitivity and courage to make the choice. I question . . . can there be safety when facing fear? I don't know."

As students struggle with facing their fears, they often seek the comfort of old, familar intellectual territories. The student with a strong arts background suddenly expresses a new defiance towards the mentor, who is the symbol of the psychological quest. She rebels, proclaiming, "I make art for the sake of making art alone. In the name of my creative integrity, all this self-analysis must stop." Students with an education or psychology background revert to old patterns of intellectualization. In either case, these theoretical retreats may be seen as defenses against the fears that emerge.

Whatever the form an individual student's resistance takes, it must be attended to by the mentor for it is a defense against the struggle that process-oriented experiential art therapy education entails. The mentor must help the student integrate the polarities of art and therapy, at the same time supporting the student's personal growth.

In optimal clinical settings there is the advantage of having the active support of the administration and the professional respect of other disciplines. In some practicum sites, art therapists are utilized as group leaders, co-therapists in psychotherapy groups, consultants to family therapists, adjuncts to psychotherapy, and in some cases, primary therapists. This is not the case in all settings, however. In some hospitals and clinics, arts therapies are viewed as little more than means for occupying time or managing client behavior. Students experience the pain of this sometimes subtle, sometimes overt devaluation of their chosen life's work as they venture out into clinical internship sites.

In the past, I have felt badly about these assaults on the art therapy profession. I have longed to protect my students from such professional cruelties. I have changed my outlook on this, however. I now see that such challenges can be viewed as opportunities art therapists are given by our fellow healers. The jabs of devaluation push students to think clearly about what they are doing and why. They are forced to think deeply about the role the arts play in the healing of suffering persons. As a mentor, I frame such painful encounters as an invaluable opportunity for the student to do one of two things: (1) attempt to foster a relationship with the devaluing colleague and eventually educate her or him about art therapy; (2) use the opportunity to learn about the practicum site's political system. It is impossible to foster change in a system without first understanding how the system functions.

Becoming part of an established institution such as a clinic or psychiatric hospital can be difficult for the student whose self-image is based upon personal freedom and creative expression. The struggle with, and sometimes against, the institutional system is a noble one, for it is a skirmish whose battleground is the soul. At some point, each of us must come to grips with how much compromising we can do without giving up our own identity. The mentor must again hold the mirror, asking the apprentice to reflect on this aspect of the journey. At the same time, the mentor seeks his own reflection and recalls the compromises and the triumphs of his own pilgrimage (Fig. 12).

I have expected the supervisors/mentors under my supervision to maintain a phenomenological approach to their students. I believe the primary role model for art therapy students best operates from a process-oriented understanding of supervision. As students become immersed in the multiplicity of communications they receive from their clients, they are often inspired and overwhelmed. Intrigued by the visual images, verbal offerings, and myriad unspoken messages generated by the client, the student must have the detached support and guidance of the mentor's ego.

The apprentice art therapist is exposed to intense rage, anguish,

Figure 12. At some point each of us must come to grips
with how much compromising we can do.

loneliness, sexuality, and the overwhelming needs of the client. For
some students, this is their first encounter with such raw power. The
mentor serves as an observing ego during the dramatic first steps of
the journey, assisting the student in filtering the multiple levels of communication. The observing ego of the supervisor assists the novice art
therapist in gaining a neutral view of subjective experiences. It has
been said that *being understood* by another is the grownup equivalent of
being held as a small child. In this way, the observing ego (mentor)
holds the intern and provides the emotional security required for the
art therapy educational experience.

Another task of the mentor in the early phases of training is the modeling of empathy. It is from an empathic stance that the supervisor is able to console the student who has committed errors of judgment. The empathic position also allows confrontation, support, and praise.

A common empathic confrontation occurs in response to students' fantasies of themselves as healers. This naive self-view is very enticing. I understand my students' desire to regard themselves as healers. I remember my own daydreams of omnipotence. I confront these issues gently with my students, for I have no wish to spoil their noble longings. Still, such images must be reframed as both admirable and unrealistic. If such fantastic self-views are not reworked in the context of supervisory sessions, they will most certainly be the source of anguish for the student when she experiences clients who refuse treatment, perceive her in a negative light, dismiss her offers of help, or even commit suicide. Clients suffering from psychiatric illness have a variety of tragic maneuvers, all of which dramatically remind the novice and seasoned practitioner alike just who is ultimately in charge of the therapy.

As students encounter the painful realities of working with clients, the mentor stands at the side, softly assuring the heroic student that she has never healed anyone and never will heal anyone. The essential paradox is that the mentor longs to heal the pain of the client and the pain of the student, but knows that all he can do is encourage both to use the creative healing power of the art process. At such times, it is most important for the supervisor to engage in his own art making, for if he only speaks of this to the student, who can believe him?

Not long ago one of my students lamented, "When I see the purple scars on that young girl's arms (her adolescent client), I ache."

I responded, "When I see you ache, I paint."

The student grumbled, "Is that all?"

I sighed, "It has to be enough."

A central theme of graduate art therapy programs must be that all feelings are acceptable, whether one is a client, a student or a therapist. We live in a culture that has separated us from the feeling process. Feelings have been categorized as "good" or "bad." Good feelings are pleasant and comfortable. Bad feelings are unpleasant and uncomfortable. Art therapy students must be encouraged to abandon this hedonistic view of feelings. Feelings are just feelings; they are amoral. Neither good nor bad, they simply *are*.

I try to emphasize that feelings are the tools of our trade, along with the whole range of art media. Just as no artist would condemn the use of any given medium, I encourage the intern to turn away from the cultural indoctrination that suggests some feelings are more worthy than others.

By focusing on the acceptability of all feelings, we free the student to bring to supervision anger towards the client, as well as pity, or disgust, or sexual attraction. Each of these *feeling responses* to clients offers growth opportunities for both the student and the client. Such growth would be impossible if the feelings themselves were repressed or denied.

The recurring theme of emptiness presented by many suffering persons seems to be difficult for students to tolerate. I have described the phenomenon of emptiness as a pervasive experience of our time (Moon, 1995). Frankl (1959) described the existential vacuum as that vague sense of boredom and desolate disinterest brought about by a lack of grounding in tradition, family, or spirituality. Due to the mobility of our society, it is common for people to be separated from hometowns, parents, and extended families. We have become a culture with little or no meaningful sense of history.

Art therapy students are not immune to these disturbing societal trends. The student cannot help but identify with the themes of loneliness, anger, and *ahistory* that bleed onto the canvas in the images of her client. She cannot help be moved by the losses depicted by her clients. Her mentor's task is to construct the boundaries she will need in her work. She must learn to separate herself from the void within her client. She cannot allow the emptiness of another to be mistaken for her own losses. At such times the skillful supervisor will share her own struggle with attachment/detachment. The student must experience the reality that the client's life does not stop when the student is not present.

I share with my students the metaphor of the guitar player. In order to play the guitar, one must develop calluses on the fingertips. Without these, the guitarist cannot play for more than a few moments. It would simply be too painful. At the same time, the calluses must not be so thick that the sense of touch is deadened. I tell the students, "If you really want to learn to do this work, you are going to have to learn to protect yourself."

Again there is an essential paradox: the art therapist must always be detached enough to be able to see clearly, yet never so detached as to be out of touch with the pain of the client. It is the same in the relationship between mentor and student. I cannot allow the student's struggles to overwhelm me, but I must always be within easy reach.

As we journey together, student and supervisor, there is a gradual transformation that takes place in the student, in me, and in our relationship. Pushed by growth beyond the bounds of naivete, through the false feelings of omnipotence, the student gains a sense of self as a professional—authentic, powerful, and humble before the creative healing force of the arts. The success of this endeavor weighs heavily on the shoulders of the supervisor/mentor. While it is true that the student is the one most responsible for the outcome, the supervisor still bears the weight of providing guidance to the traveler.

Chapter VII

THE ART EXPERIENCE

The Seventh Essential–In order to be an art therapist, you must engage in the art process at a deep level.

In a videotaped interview with Don Jones, one of the American pioneers of creative arts therapy, the question was asked, "Are you an artist or a therapist?" His response was emphatic, "I am an artist." In the nearly thirty years that I have known Don, his answer has never changed. "I AM AN ARTIST." There are no doubt others who contributed to the birth of the profession would answer in a similar way. However, there was a period of time when in our history when art therapists seemed to lack the passion of this conviction. In the 1990s, the fiery dedication to an identity as an artist seemed as if it had cooled.

I was once teaching a course at an institute where this question became a source of controversy. I declared that art therapists needed to remain active in their own artistic media in order to preserve their authenticity as art therapists. A student who was very near graduation spoke, "Are you saying that the art therapist has to be able to paint in order to be genuine in their work?"

"No," I replied, "that is not exactly what I mean. You can paint, or sculpt, or write, or dance—whatever. The medium you choose is up to you. My point is that in order to be an art therapist, you must engage in the art process at a deep level."

The student recoiled. "I don't think I like this idea very much. It seems to me it is most important that I am a good therapist who understands the theories of personality and the principles of psychotherapy. I use the art as a vehicle for relating, but I am certainly no artist in my own right."

I responded, "If the art is only an ancillary process to your therapy work, why bother calling what you do art therapy?"

Over the years, I have had similar exchanges with my peers at regional and national art therapy conferences. It is a troublesome issue at this time within the American Art Therapy Association. In fact, until very recently, the standards for graduate art therapy educational programs generated by the American Art Therapy Association did not support continued engagement in studio art coursework. In 1992, when the first edition of this text was published, studio art courses were mentioned only in passing as possible electives. However, I am pleased to report the Education Standards that became effective in July of 2002, now list studio art as a required content area for master's degree programs.

There is a longstanding sarcastic comment about educators that goes like this: those who can, do; those who can't, teach. As an art therapist, educator, and artist, I respond to this notion at several levels. It is essential for art therapy educators to remain active in their clinical work. It is not enough to review the literature with the student. One must be able to speak from an expert position based in active therapeutic work. At the same time, it is crucial for art therapy educators to continue our own artistic growth and work. At still another level, educators are committed to teaching in the field. It is the only way we have of repaying the mentors of our lives. By remaining focused on my art, therapy, and education identity, I bring honor to my teachers.

The students who come to art therapy programs need to engage actively in art processes. It is not enough that they practice art as a form of parallel play in the presence of clients. They must make art for themselves and about themselves. In the early days of the Harding Graduate Clinical Art Therapy Program, Don Jones devised a series of 20 art tasks that the student was expected to complete during the training year. He called this, *the artist's life script.* As the program evolved, the life script format was abandoned for a more open, less prescriptive studio requirement.

The journey that the creative arts therapy student makes is a complex one. The student travels many paths at once. One path is filled with articles, books, and lectures. One is strewn with emotional landmines, booby traps planted in the unconscious by encounters with clients. Yet another is an inward path, shaped through the integrating creative art experience. It is on this inner road that the tired and battered student may find rest and comfort.

It is nearly inevitable that students come to a crisis point in their

Figure 13. Go into the studio and make art.

long training journey. I suspect that nearly all arts therapists experience a similar difficult period in their professional lives. The precipitating factors are as varied as the individuals themselves. The common characteristics of the crisis are that motivations are questioned, confidence is shaken, and stability is disrupted. It is at this point in graduate school and in practice that the arts processes are needed most. All too often, however, it is precisely during these periods that many students withdraw from their own art making. It is as if they believe that to engage in creative work would steal what precious energy they still possess.

Whether the crisis is brought on through intense relating with seriously ill clients, or difficult and frustrating work settings, or by the unrelenting work load of graduate school, or by personal relationships outside of the educational setting, my counsel is always the same: Get back into the studio and MAKE ART (Fig. 13).

Several years ago, an art therapy alumnus from a program where I had taught called to share that he was going through a difficult time in his life. After leaving the graduate program, he had gone on to become the art therapist on the psychiatric wing of a large metropolitan general hospital. Three years later, he secured a job with a state agency and was promoted to a high administrative post. His promotion had taken him entirely away from clinical contact with the clients the agency served. He asked if we might get together to talk things over. I suggested we meet for dinner early the next week.

As we ate, he explained in detail the many changes in his life since my last contact with him. He had married, bought a house, and now was the father of a son. His job paid well, almost twice what I earned that year. Still, he was discontent. He talked for most of an hour. I listened, nodded my head, and commented now and then. When at last he seemed to run down, I asked, "When was the last time you did any sculpture, or painted?" (One of my clearest memories of him was of his hands covered with paint.)

He sighed, "Bruce, who has the time?" For the rest of our dinner, I prodded, cajoled, and coaxed him to get back to the studio.

A few months later he called me again. He said that he was quite depressed and asked if I could recommend a private practice therapist for him to go see. I gave him the name of a therapist I respected a great deal. As he was about to hang up, I asked, "By the way, have you done any art work lately?"

There was a long pause. "Well, I tried. Every time I started a painting, though, I couldn't stand what I was painting. It was horrible. So I quit trying."

In his book, *Depth Psychology of Art*, McNiff (1989) argues that the purpose of artists is to awaken to consciousness the experience of soul. It is impossible for art making to happen without deep psychological stirrings happening as well. This is not to say that all artists would be willing to imagine themselves as depth psychologists, nor would many have the desire to verbalize these stirrings. Still, I contend that there is soul-work taking place, consciously acknowledged or not. I think this accounts for my graduate's resistance to painting. For a variety of reasons, he did not want to be moved by his own creative forces.

The heroes and heroines of fairy-tale journeys must go through times of darkness and deep isolation. In mythology, this is known as the time of ashes, a time of descent. The heroic one is helped along the way by primitive things—a stone or a wild animal. Although the heroic one may feel utterly lost and alone, he or she is eventually guided back to the light, but helped only when help is most needed.

Training to be an art therapist is a deep experience. To engage with

Figure 14. I guess I painted my way home.

one's art and the art of others exerts a powerful inward pull, toward the core of the self. Images born during the training years, particularly in crisis periods, are manifestations of the soul-work in process. As a profession, we cannot afford to stray too far from our soul–ART. I am saddened when I hear my colleagues confess that they have not worked in their own media seriously since they started their 40-hour-a-week jobs, or since they got married, or since their children were born. If we fail to make use of the art process for ourselves, the cre-

Figure 15.

ative spirit of art therapists may eventually dry up and be blown away like dust.

As a mentor, as a peer, I encourage my students to work with their art. I applaud their having stained hands. I urge them not to be ashamed of the paint smears on their shirts. I do this in every way I know how. I am there in the time of dark isolation. I carry a flashlight and a sketchpad. I share stories of my own journey. When they ask me how I survived the perils of my dark caverns, I tell them the truth: *I don't know, I guess I painted my way home* (Figs. 14 & 15).

Chapter VIII

THE CORE CURRICULUM

The Eighth Essential—We must educate our students to become masters of the discipline.

The number of high quality graduate art therapy training programs has expanded dramatically over the past 30 years. There has also been a substantial increase in the volume of written materials about the art therapy profession. When I was a beginning student, I was frustrated that there was so little I could find to read about this new and exciting field. Today's graduate students need not feel so deprived. *The Journal of the American Art Therapy Association, The American Journal of Art Therapy,* and *The Arts in Psychotherapy Journal* have done much to disseminate information that has deepened and enriched the fund of knowledge. Added to those publications have been the significant works of many textbook authors. Finally, the efforts of the American Art Therapy Association to publish and record proceedings of annual conferences have provided a wealth of information now available to student and practitioner alike.

The availability of all this information has had a curious effect upon the professional identity of art therapists. What is most important in the education of art therapists and the practice of art therapy has been the subject of much discussion. What are the boundaries of the art therapy profession? How do art therapy principles apply to non-treatment situations? Shall we regard ourselves as artists first, artists who use their natural sensitivity to humanity? Or shall we think of ourselves as psychotherapists who use the arts as an adjunct in our work with clients?

Don Jones often described himself as an artist who worked with the emotionally disturbed. Harriett Wadeson (1980) stated, "Art therapists should be psychotherapists plus" (p. 24). This orientation question may seem to split semantic hairs and there are some present-day art therapists who regard this question as irrelevant. I believe, however, that the ongoing struggle with this question has deep and lasting influence on the future of the profession.

Educators must decide the type of professional to be shaped through graduate art therapy education. Are we educating psychotherapists who dabble in paint and clay, or are we shaping a unique profession in which art processes and products are ascribed weight equal to developmental theory, psychotherapeutic technique, and abnormal psychology? These questions have become even more profound over the last several years as more and more art therapists seek employment outside of traditional health and mental health care institutional settings.

I have passionate responses to these questions. The depth and power of artistic, creative self-expression suggests that engaging in art processes can be a significant learning experience. The art therapist must be sensitive to the pushes and pulls of line character, the ebb and flow of emotional currents affected by color, and the potentialities of weight, mass, and emptiness in form. Artistic sensitivities are then coupled with academic understanding of human development, psychological theory, individual, group and family dynamics, community organization, as well as systems of counseling and psychotherapy.

It is critical that educators of art therapists resist the seduction of teaching their students to be as-if psychologists or pseudo-counselors. The political pressures generated by state licensure boards and third-party payers should not provide the impetus for programs to educate students to become counselors who doodle or social workers who play with chalk.

Students who want to become art therapists have a right to be educated as art therapists and nothing less. Students who long to be verbal psychotherapists should seek the recognized routes to that end. If they want to be marital therapists, they should be encouraged to enter social work or counseling programs that emphasize marital therapy. The professional identity of the art therapist must lie in the equal weighting of both words contained in the discipline's name: ART and THERAPY.

To adopt a polarized view, whether valuing art over therapy or therapy over art, is to take a path toward weakening the integrity of the art therapy profession. These elements are the *yin* and *yang* of who we are. They cannot be separated and they should not be presented in ways that value one over the other.

During the past 20 years, much discussion in the American Art Therapy Association has revolved around issues of professionalism. The hierarchy of health and mental health institutions generally places physicians/psychiatrists at the top level, followed by nurses, psychologists, and social workers. In our history, awareness of such hierarchies led some art therapists to attempt to emulate these disciplines. These efforts were based upon the notion that professional worth is measured by the accumulation of institutional power and personal income. That kind of measurement is discomforting to me. I am unwilling to judge an art therapist's work on the basis of tax bracket or hourly fee.

Still, the lure of imitating these professions is a powerful one. We have to come to grips with the reality that our professional prestige must come from within our own profession. This is not so easy. The first problem is one of definition: what exactly is an art therapist? Breaking the title down to its components is not much help. The debate over "what is art?" is centuries old. When I refer to art, and therefore to arts therapists, I am referring to painting, sculpture, drawing, poetry, music, dance, and drama. Art has to do with the intent to express some essential aspect of human existence. One of the best attempts at defining art I ever heard came from a client who suggested that art is "like a window to the soul" (Fig. 16). This, however, leaves one looking for definitions of soul.

We know that the word *therapy* is derived from the greek, *therapeuticus*, which means to be attentive to. What does it mean to be attentive to the windows of the soul?

We begin to grasp the problems of professional identity. Science has taught people to distrust their senses. For example, the earth moves around the sun. In a non-scientific age, humans looked up at the sky and watched the sun move past them from sunrise to noon, to dusk and finally to night. Their senses told them that the sun moves. They did not feel, or see, or hear the earth move. They watched the sun. What else was to be believed? The earth is still, the sun moves. Science has taught us that it is the Earth that moves and the sun is still. Science has taught us to be skeptical of what we perceive through our senses. The art therapy profession is integrally linked to the senses. Whether of sight or sound or touch, the arts engage the senses.

It is important to remind ourselves that the root word of *psyche* is *soul*. Where, one may ask, does the soul reside? The problems of def-

Figure 16. Like a window to the soul.

inition of our profession are exacerbated if and when we describe ourselves as *art psychotherapists*. One root-oriented definition might be, "one who skillfully attends to the windows of the soul." While I personally like this definition, I can easily imagine colleagues screaming their protestations that this is no definition at all.

We are in a curious situation at this time regarding the mind-body split. Clearly such divisions remain in our culture. We do see evidence of some resurgence of a more unified view of humanity, however. Still, the perception of a gulf between psyche and soma persists. Feder and Feder (1981) comment, "The relationship between mind and body is acknowledged in modern medicine, but is almost always expressed as psychosomatic, rather than somatopsychic."

The arts, however, have resurfaced as a treatment for a wide variety of emotional, mental, and physical disorders. Inevitably, the recognition that mind, body, and spirit are interconnected has led to increased interest in the creative arts and other non-verbal therapies. There are many clients for whom traditional verbal psychiatric treatment is either inappropriate or unavailable. Informed providers of mental health treatment are facing the reality that some people do not retain auditory stimuli; that some people do not learn through dialogue; that verbalized insight is useless if not translated into meaningful action (Fig. 17).

Art therapy graduate educational programs have struggled with a daunting task. On the one hand, in many places, it is necessary to conform to educational criteria for various state licenses while, on the other hand, attempting to maintain focus on the unique aspects of art therapy practice. As an educator, I believe it is important to return to the roots of the art therapy profession. The task is to educate professional art therapists, people who do good work for the sake of their clients' well-being. My work is to help students on the journey to becoming "one who skillfully attends to the windows of the soul."

The core curriculum of graduate art therapy programs consists of art therapy history, art therapy theory, techniques of practice, application of art therapy with people in different treatment and community settings, awareness of multicultural issues, art therapy assessment, ethical and legal issues of art therapy practice, standards of practice, and a thesis or thesis equivalent. Within the curriculum, students are exposed to psychopathology and diagnostics, human growth and development, group dynamics, research methodologies, and studio art. The core curriculum also includes supervised practical experience and opportunities for specialization in art therapy competency areas.

A graduate student asked me to suggest a reading list, explaining that she felt inadequate in designing art therapy exercises. "I just don't know how to think metaphorically," she said. I suggested that she read *Grimm's Fairy Tales*, Camus' *The Fall*, Melville's *Moby Dick*, Robert Frost, D. H. Lawrence, Bruno Bettelheim, J. D. Salinger, W. P. Kinsella, E.E. cummings, Joseph Campbell, Robert Bly, John Donne, Kurt Vonnegut, Stephen King, Toni Morrison, et cetera.

My point, though exaggerated, was that literature, classic and contemporary, prose and poetry, profound and popular, is the best source of therapeutic metaphor. Literature is an interpretation of life as experienced by the artist/author. The creative arts therapist, whose task is to respond sensitively to the art (life interpretations) of the client, needs a repertoire of literary, musical, visual, and sensual memories from which to draw her responses. We run the risk of becoming too narrow in our thinking if we restrict the fields of inquiry to readings in art therapy and psychology.

Figure 17. Insight is useless if not translated into meaningful action.

An analogy may be made to the specialties in auto repair. I go to one place to have my muffler fixed, another to have the brakes adjusted. Someone else takes care of the tires and another mechanic works on engine repairs. Oil changes are done at the gas station, but when my radio quit working, it had to be sent to a service center three states away. With all that, the car still doesn't run very well and I have the uneasy feeling that no one in the world understands how an entire automobile functions.

The creative arts therapies are related not only to psychology and art, but to philosophy, community activism, theology, and literature—all the humanities as well. Graduate programs might review course content with an eye towards integrating studio art and these other human studies.

Chapter IX

THE PRACTICAL EXPERIENCE

The Ninth Essential–The student must have a significant period of time to work consistently with clients.

I do not recall exactly when I read my first description of mental illness. It might have been in high school when I discovered *I Never Promised You A Rose Garden* (Green, 1964) in Senior English. Or it might have been in Psychology 101 at Bowling Green State University in Ohio. Whenever, wherever it was, I remember the sense of awe and fascination I felt as I read about schizophrenia, depression, and anxiety disorders. The more I learned, the more I was captivated. I read and read and read, all the while seeking degrees in art education, theology, and education, areas that had little obvious connection with mental illness.

I had heard of art therapy from my faculty advisor, Dr. Gary Barlowe at Wright State University, but I had not considered it as a possible vocation until I became a student at the Methodist Theological School in Delaware, Ohio. I had intended to become a pastor who specialized in counseling ministry. While in graduate school, I was hired by the Worthington Community Counseling service, a treatment program for adolescents. My job description was not very specific. Somehow I was to relate to troubled teenagers through music and the visual arts, provide evening and weekend telephone counseling, drop-in crisis intervention, and suicide hotline counseling.

With the naive courage of the young, I was confident that all of my reading and coursework had prepared me well for this position. I was sure that I was equal to the task. I would not disappoint the center's director. Since he had faith in me, I was secure, though a novice.

My first client appeared on my second night on duty. She was not an adolescent, but she was quite troubled. Her hair was a wild, uncombed tangle. She smelled badly from days without a bath. Her eyes darted around the office. When I asked her to sit down, she recoiled and flattened her body against the door.

Client: "No, my God, no! Do you think I am just going to walk in here and do anything you want me to?

Bruce: "Well, of course not. I just thought you'd be more comfortable sitting down. Can I be of help?"

Client: "You can make them leave me alone."

Bruce: "Whom are you talking about?"

Client: "The thugs at the halfway house."

She lit a cigarette and began to circle the room. My mind raced, filled with anxiety: *This woman is frightening me. She's not supposed to be here. I'm only supposed to talk with kids. What halfway house? What thugs? What's she going to do with me? I wish she'd sit down. Why am I here alone? I should have taken that teaching job. My God, what do I do?*

Eventually the woman did calm down. She was able to telephone the psychiatric halfway house where she was a resident. They sent a staff member over to pick her up and return her to the house. Later I learned that she was suffering with paranoid schizophrenia and that she had episodes like this every now and then. She had been to most of the community counseling centers in the city at one time or another.

This information was of little use to me. I was angry with myself because I had panicked. I had been unable to think clearly and had not had a clue as to how best to help the woman, even though her behavior was straight out of the textbook. That was when I learned that reading about a psychiatric disorder is very different from being in the presence of a human being who has that disorder.

This incident, illuminating the difference between the clinical description and living reality, illustrates why clinical experience is essential for art therapy students. Regarding practical art therapy experience and supervision, the education standards of the American Art Therapy Association state that each student must be required to successfully complete a minimum of seven hundred (700) hours of supervised art therapy practice. In at least 350 hours of the supervised practice, the student must be working directly with patients [clients] in individual, group, or family formats. The balance of the supervised hours must include discussion of student work with the supervisor(s) and related activities. These discussions and related activities may include case review, record keeping, preparation, and staff meetings.

Supervision of the practicum experience may take place on- or off-site.

Art therapy supervision can take one of two forms. The first is individual supervision in which, for every 10 hours of client contact, there must be one hour of supervision by a registered art therapist (ATR). The second form of supervision is group supervision. A ratio of eight students to one ATR supervisor may not be exceeded for group supervision. There must be two hours of group supervision for every 10 hours of client contact. For every 10 hours of related activity, there must be one hour of supervision by either a registered art therapist or a qualified professional with at least a master's degree in a related discipline.

At first glance, the AATA education standards appear to expect that educational programs include meaningful clinical experience as a component of the educational program. However, looking deeper, these standards are disturbing. I am particularly uneasy about the 700 hours of supervised art therapy experience. When 700 hours are spread over a two-year (four semester) period, this averages out to roughly three hours a day. Presumably as many as half of those three hours can be spent in "related activities," leaving only one and a half hour per day being spent with clients doing art therapy. Now, I know this is a worst-case scenario, but in such a practicum, there is little opportunity for a consistent, integrated experience for the student. It might even be worse to have the student at a practicum site for only two days a week but for more hours each day. If that were the case, the student would be able to get a better feel for the flow of a given day, but would have no opportunity to experience the flow of a week or a month at the site.

Healthcare institutions have a life and rhythm of their own. It is important for students to learn how to be a part of the system. The value of internship experiences is that creative arts therapy is taught in the context of practical reality. Through practical experience, art therapy students learn the role their discipline plays in the milieu. They must also come to understand the roles of colleagues from other disciplines. Only when one understands all the components of the milieu can one understand and articulate one's own unique contribution to the client. Consistent, sustained experience in the practicum setting gives students the opportunity to develop and articulate an understanding of the contributions of art therapy to the helping professions.

Artistic Encounters in the Clinical Setting

When we approach the canvas as artists, or the client as art therapists, we bring all of our experience and knowledge to the encounter. Yet, once there, we must let go of past biases or worries about the future in order to be genuinely in the present. I have stressed to my students the importance of full concentration while in art therapy sessions with clients. The students cannot be distracted by worries outside the therapy encounter. It is important for students to learn to bracket worries in order to focus attention on clients. It is essential that art therapists be nowhere else than in the present when doing therapy.

In order to understand the nature of this intense *here and now* creative encounter, it is helpful to turn to the art process itself as a metaphor of the experience. The artistic encounter may best be examined through the analogous observation of the artist in the inspirational phase of creative work. The artist loses all sense of past and future, existing only in the present moment. Totally absorbed, fascinated, and immersed in the here and now task, the artist is *all there.*

The willingness and capacity to be locked into the present seems to be a fundamental attribute for creative action. It may be described as a loss of ego, or more positively, as a transcendence of self. In artistic activity there is a sense of integration, a fusion of sorts between the artist and the media. Regardless of art form—paint, dance, music, or rhyme—some artists describe a sense of ecstatic revelation and bliss (Moon, 1997).

Don Jones (2000) has described his artistic experiences as *epiphanies.* Others have referred to them as peak experiences. Whether we regard them as natural psychological events or extraordinary human processes, the common characteristics seem to be a complete and compelling fascination with the task at hand. Such depictions of the focal processes of art have much to offer in enriching our understanding of artistic and therapeutic encounters with clients.

The Artist. As the painter moves her brush from palette to canvas, she is aware that she has done the same motions before. She is aware that she has used the medium before and perhaps employed the same color combinations in earlier works. In this sense, her past is a part of her. It is assimilated throughout her being. Yet, she cannot paint again what she painted before. To do so would lead to frustration and estrangement from the work before her. She must give up the past; she must let it go in order to be with the canvas that is now (Fig. 18).

Figure 18. Be with the canvas that is now.

The Art Therapist. I allow memories of past encounters with clients to be in the current session only in the sense that these are integrated, digested aspects of self. The intervention so effective with one client last week may have little or no therapeutic benefit to the client present today.

Artist. As the painter works, she cannot afford to look too far ahead in the process. To do so would be to become oblivious to the emerging image in the present. The moment must be allowed to stand for its own sake, not solely as a springboard to some future process.

Art Therapist. The same is true within the therapeutic creative encounter. In order to be effective, I attend to what the client is doing now, rather than hypothesizing what might happen in the next session. In an existential sense, there is no next session; there is only the present one. In a realistic, pragmatic sense, there may be no next time. I must be an agent for good in the current moment.

Artist. As the artist paints, she attempts to work without guile, to be oblivious to what should, or ought, to be happening. If she is success-

Figure 19. She cannot afford to look too far ahead.

ful, the interaction between self and image dictates the moment, not some dogmatic rule. There is a sense of childlike innocence or purity of intent that may be likened to standing naked. She is receptive to the moment without manipulation or demand.

Art Therapist. I have often felt childlike and even foolish in the early stages of therapy. Often clients will test my intentions. Doing therapy is an opening of oneself, a making vulnerable to another, which is foolishness in the best sense of the word. Within the artistic therapeutic encounter, the therapist must bring positive regard for the other's well-being.

Artist. As images begin to form on the canvas, the artist may become less aware of outside influences. She becomes fully focused on the canvas. She abandons her public facades, forgetting her desires to influence others, to gain recognition and to win approval. Through the artistic process, she is able to be herself, genuinely, authentically. With no distractions, she is able to attach herself completely to the task of painting.

Figure 20. There is no next session.

Art Therapist. I usher the client in and close the door to the studio. I can feel my customary social masks begin to loosen. I take my customary position in the room and feel one of my masks fall away completely. My client begins to draw and another pulls away from my face. For the next 50 minutes I have no audience, no one to act for, no one to please. With no script to read from and no theme to improvise from, I am free to be with my client genuinely. I devote myself to her drama.

Artist. As images continue to form, the artist may become caught up in the birth within her and without. She does not critique or edit, nor does she reject or judge. She just lets the paint flow.

Art Therapist. As the client works, I become absorbed in her process. I watch her and am with her. I do not cut her off or analyze. I do not interpret or evaluate. I just let the session flow.

Artist. The artist may step back from the painting to get a broader look at the work in progress. She tries not to indulge in worrying about what others will say in regard to the piece. She attempts not to censor the work for the sake of acceptance. There may be an air of stubborn self-confidence. The necessary acceptance comes from within her, not from outside. In the creative moment, there can be an intrinsic uninhibited, defenseless, genuine quality. Fear and indecision are forsaken, replaced by an inner strength and courage. Such artistic, self-absorbed courage allows the artist to be open to the mysterious, ambiguous, and paradoxical. Courage paves the way to action.

Art Therapist. My client, a 15-year-old adolescent girl steps away from the image she has created. Tears slide down her cheeks. I look in awe at the scene of a little five-year-old girl being abused by a malevolent babysitter. I am horrified and appalled, but I must face this monstrous image with stubborn, open courage. If I show the slightest fear or revulsion, she may well misinterpret it as judgment of her. I will not indulge my fear. It is the enemy of creativity. For the moment, I will be with this little girl and we will be strong and courageous together. We will look at this painful image with stubborn confidence. We will not be intimidated anymore.

Artist. Positive and optimistic, the artist may pick up the brush again and move back towards the canvas. She accepts the image being born. She lets it be itself. She is receptive and humble and she lets the process have its own way.

Art Therapist. As my clients bring their images to the studio, revealing them in paint or chalk or clay, I make every effort to approve and bring honor to the unveiling. I maintain an attitude of awe in the company of client artistry. I accept their offerings and in every way I can imagine, I ennoble them. Regardless of the visual form, I attempt to affirm the validity of the creative struggle.

Figure 21. We will look at this.

Artist. The artist paints, striving to trust the process. She waits, quietly receptive. Willing to forgo the desire to master and control, she has faith in the process.

Art Therapist. Many times in my life, I have felt a need to dominate or be in control. Excessive focus on mastery or technique has affected my golf swing, my teaching, and supervisory responsibilities, and most certainly my therapy sessions. I have had to learn to relax and trust the process. I learned to float on my back in water as soon as I quit flailing about. Likewise I am a much more effective art therapist when I abandon my attempts to control the therapy. I trust the process.

Artist. Suddenly the gray-green bleeds into the burnt sienna. The artist watches the accident, and then gently, instinctually works in concert with the unexpected. She had not intended for this to happen, but her capacity to adapt to the situation at hand allows her to use the accident in a positive, nearly effortless, intuitive way. She does not allow the bleeding to become a battleground.

Art Therapist. As an art therapist, I strive to concentrate so completely upon the task before me, with such fascination and awe, that I

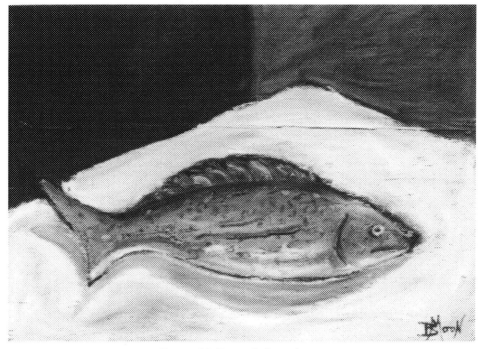

Figure 22. I quit flailing about.

can function both thoughtfully and spontaneously. My competencies promote flexibility, as the situation demands, while I continuously adapt to the weight of the here-and-now encounter. As the waters of an ocean adapt to the continuously shifting contours of the shore, so I rely on my intuition to enable me to flow with the process.

* * *

Art therapy educators can provide educational environments that promote students' artistic epiphanies, ecstasies, and peak experiences. When educators model authentic engagement in the creative encounter, students are likely inspired to engage their own artwork in a meaningful way. A three-pronged approach in the educational environment is ideal. First, the teacher/supervisor/mentor teaches by example. The instructor not only describes experiences to the class, but also provides opportunities for the students to have experiences in the context of the class. Second, educational programs integrate art processes into the learning environment as a way to process students' experiences in the practicum setting. Studio art courses may be offered

as part of the curriculum, along with art therapy or psychology courses that integrate art making into class experiences and assignments.
Finally, students in the clinical setting need to receive appropriate
supervisory support that emphasizes the essential nature of the therapy hour as a creative and artistic encounter.

Chapter X

SCIENCE AND SOUL IN
THE CLINICAL SETTING

**The Tenth Essential–The special gift of the creative arts
therapies to the client and to the clinical setting is
the soul/art-making process.**

In the 1990s, psychiatric hospitals, general hospitals, community
mental health agencies, and clinical treatment settings of all types
underwent massive changes in response to the demands of health
maintenance organizations, third-party payers, and increased competition. Advances made in bio-neurological understandings of emotional disorders and in the treatment of mental disorders also affected the
nature of care provided in clinical settings. Over the course of a
decade, the average length of stay for clients in inpatient medical and
psychiatric hospitals, both private and state run, dropped dramatically. When I began my career as an art therapist in 1974, the average
length of stay for inpatients at the hospital where I was employed was
approximately nine months. It was not atypical for patients to stay for
over a year. When I left the hospital in 1996, the average length of stay
was down to five or six days. As a result, much of the language of therapists has shifted from the poetic, abstract, and qualitative toward the
functional, concrete, and quantifiable. One counselor recently confid-
ed, "I no longer talk about feelings with my clients. We only talk about
goals that can be measured in observable behavioral terms."

I have expressed my firm belief that what we do as art therapists
cannot be measured in purely quantitative terms (Moon 1990). McNiff
(1989) asserts that we must reclaim our roots in a view of the arts as an
"unconscious religion," and turn with all due respect away from over-
scientification of our field (pp. 19–25). Another colleague, Sr. Kathleen
Burke of Ursuline College, has expressed concern over the increasing
popularity of assessment procedures used by arts therapists. Her con-

cern is that this trend reflects an attempt to concretize and quantify arts phenomena, thus shifting art therapists' roles toward technical formulaic interpretation of images and away from soulful practice.

Art therapists are not alone in this identity struggle. Psychiatrists, psychologists, social workers, and others in the helping professions raise similar concerns. Speaking clearly about this dilemma is the noted psychologist and prolific author James Hillman. In the first pages of his work, *Re-Visioning Psychology* (Hillman, 1975), he writes:

> This book is about soul making. It is an attempt at a psychology of soul, an essay in re-visioning psychology from the point of view of soul. This book is therefore old-fashioned and radically novel because it harks back to the classical notions of soul and yet advances ideas that current psychology has not even begun to consider. (p. ix)

Professionals at all levels within clinical settings have experienced an identity crisis and a crisis of conscience. We have been forced to examine critically who we are and what we do in the service of our clients. Our sense of integrity has been battered by the reality of a severely limited financial system in which the determinant of quality care given has been seriously compromised by the dictates of faceless insurance reviewers.

Still, the clinical setting is an essential milieu for meaningful education in the creative arts therapies. Therefore, it is imperative that attention is given the student in relation to the dichotomy of science and soul in clinical settings. Not only do educators have a responsibility to the student in this regard, but the student has an important role as well. The student's task is to question why things are the way they are.

In a group supervision session, one of my graduate students was struggling with this issue. She reported having attended a psychiatric team meeting during which members of the team were bemoaning the "negative attention-seeking behaviors" of a particular client. One of the staff members commented, "This woman just needs to take her meds and get out of here."

Another member of the team had chimed in, "Yes, we don't have time to deal with her games."

The student was taken aback by the derogatory tone of the discussion. In an attempt to shift the tenor of the conversation, she spoke up. "In the arts studio she [the client] is really struggling with some painful memory images from the past."

Figure 23. Treating the whole person.

One of the nurses responded, "That's all well and good, but we are not really here to work through all that old stuff."

The student replied, "But aren't we supposed to be treating the whole person? Isn't that why we call the treatment plan a bio-psycho-social plan?"

The team leader countered, "I don't want to sound coldhearted, but the bottom line is she needs to take her medications and the pressure is on for us to get her out of here by the end of the week!"

In the supervision session, the student wrestled with her sense of responsibility to the client, juxtaposed against the realities the team was facing in regards to the client's course of treatment.

It is evident that the student was not really in a position to change the way the system worked at that treatment facility. In all likelihood, none of the members of the treatment team had influence over the system that determined reimbursement limitations for the clients they served either. Still, I think it is important for students to question such realities. Students' questions may spark a dialogue among therapists that can rekindle courage in the face of a health care system that is wrestling with its soul. There really is more to mental and physical therapy than physiology and finance.

I am wary about the scientification of the helping professions in general and arts therapy in particular. I fear that by attempting to align our teaching of art processes too closely to the methods of science, we run the risk of pathologizing the arts. Likewise, if art therapy education focuses exclusively on teaching art therapy techniques or assessment procedures likely to qualify for third-party reimbursement, the soul of the profession is endangered. Superficial psychological inquiries in relation to the works of artists can be damaging. Some works on the lives of Van Gogh, Camille Claudel, Picasso, Pollack and others, have given the public the misguided notion that the arts are the realm of lunatics.

On the other hand, if arts therapies in the clinical training setting are approached from a perspective of *soul,* the work becomes sacred. While I embrace the concept that art comes from the depth of human beings, out of turmoil and conflict and passion, I believe art making is inherently a healthy process, not pathological ventilation.

Having expressed my reservations regarding scientification, I feel compelled to assure the reader that I am not really anti-science, especially when science is related to human well-being. Who can question the near-miraculous benefit of lithium to persons suffering from bipolar disorder? Who doubts the positive contributions of bio-neurology in the treatment of schizophrenia? My point is not to devalue science, but to bring honor to the intuitive, soul-making processes of the arts. By suggesting that art making is soul making, I mean that art processes offer a new perspective. Painting, dancing, and writing makes meaning possible by turning arbitrary occurrences into deep experiences. There is an artistic foundation to human existence and a perspective that cannot be pinpointed as the property of behavior or language or society or brain physiology. The special gift of the creative arts therapies to the client and to the clinical setting is this soul/art-making process.

It is essential that art therapy educational programs not only impart mechanics of the profession, but philosophical underpinnings as well. When attention is given to both the science and the soul of art therapy, the student is prepared to understand the treatment of individuals and groups, and also the functions of systems, hierarchy, and political issues that are integral within mental health and health care institutions. It is important for art therapists to understand both pragmatic and philosophic aspects of their life's work.

Chapter XI

THE WORK OF ART THERAPY

**The Eleventh Essential–Becoming an art therapist
requires effort, strain, purposeful toil, and the ability
to be patient and passionate.**

Lou Powers, whose journal entries were included in an earlier chapter of this book, is a graduate of the Harding Graduate Clinical Art Therapy Program and the Expressive Therapy Graduate Program at Lesley University. Shortly after she returned from a five-week summer intensive at the Lesley campus, Lou shared with me the joy of the relationships she had made there and the relief and satisfaction that accompanied the completion of her master's thesis. Lou's face glowed as she told me of her friends and the experiences she'd had in the Boston area.

I commented, "It sounds like a wonderful time, Lou. It must have been fun."

Her expression changed immediately. She said, "It was very hard work." An awkward silence hung between us briefly. The intensity of this sudden shift in the emotional tone in our conversation heightened my awareness of just how hard the work of becoming an art therapist is for students and teachers.

"Lou," I said, "you've only just begun. Being an art therapist is hard work too."

Webster's (1988) defines work as "physical or mental effort exerted to do or make something; purposeful activity, labor, toil . . . to strain . . . to cause or bring about . . . to cultivate, to cause to function . . . to ferment . . ." (p. 1538).

The work of learning to be, being, and teaching about being an art therapist is strenuous, straining, purposeful toil. It is not easy.

Joseph Campbell (1988) describes the image of the *warrior* as one who is able to discipline his efforts and follow his bliss. By his own description, Campbell lived the warrior role through disciplined inquiry into the myths of numerous cultures, at times reading eight to ten hours a day. He exemplified *passionate discipline.*

Perhaps passionate discipline is an apt description of the work involved in becoming an art therapist. Here again a reference to the artistic process is relevant. The products of our artistic endeavors are described as *art works,* or *works of art.* No one would dare to look at the Sistine Chapel and marvel over Michaelangelo's *avocational* pursuits. It is his *work!* As fanciful and playful as Calder's mobiles may appear, few would question the work they required.

When reviewing the retrospective work of any artist, one comes to grips with the sum of his or her effort, the strain and purposeful toil involved and the ability of the artist to be patient and passionate as the work proceeded throughout the years. One senses the artist's willingness to tolerate internal storms and fermentations. One finds traces and hints of the physical effort demanded by the art. The work of the artist is not easy, resulting in blisters–both physical and emotional–tired muscles, cramped fingers, and weary eyes. The life's work of an artist is a testament that the struggle was worth it, that it mattered.

Such "mattering" must lie at the core of the student, practitioner and teacher. The art therapy profession demands passionate discipline and faith in the struggle. Judy Rubin (1984) comments on this aspect of the work in *The Art of Art Therapy:*

> It is possible to master the art of many things, such as piano playing, gourmet cooking, crewel embroidery and to do them well . . . but to do them in such a way that people sigh when they hear one's sonatas, or eat one's mousse, or view one's wall hangings requires something above and beyond the mastery of the art form itself–something best identified as artistry.

What Rubin calls artistry, I would describe as passionate discipline. The misinformed may speak of works of art as the product of genius or talent. While certainly gifts and talent may have a role in the development of artistry, I recall Powers' statement, "It was very hard work." No artist can rely solely upon genius to produce. The artist must do the work. So it is with art therapists. There are surely some students who bring to the training experience intrinsic characteristics of wholesomeness, health, and warmth. These inherent qualities alone are not enough to produce an art therapist. As Rubin notes, "being an artist and a nice human being is not enough to make someone a good art therapist" (p. 67). Intellectual capacity is not enough, nor artistic sensibility, nor concern for humankind. None of these attributes are sufficient in isolation. The would-be art therapist must bring a passionate discipline that will patiently blend charisma, warmth, artistic perspective, skill, love for humanity and intellect with a willingness to work.

In the transition from undergraduate to graduate work, an intriguing transformation often occurs in the student. In undergraduate school, there are inevitably courses and assignments a student must undertake in order to proceed with his or her education, even if the courses are not of interest to the student. These are, in some measure, hoops to be jumped through. The student recognizes them as such when they are encountered. Such hoops inspire less than excellent work. In fact, they encourage half-hearted efforts to get by and move on.

Graduate school, however, presents the student with an environment dedicated to the individual student's personal investment in his or her own excellence. Graduate school marks a shift from academic hoop jumping. Students transform their sense of identity as hoop-jumping performers for faculty approval to dedicated colleagues of master practitioners. This is not an easy transition to make, but the work of becoming an art therapist demands it.

In an interview published by Giovanni Papini (1934) Sigmund Freud is quoted:

> Everybody thinks that I stand by the scientific character of my work and that my principal scope lies in curing mental maladies. This is terrible error that has prevailed for years and that I have been unable to set right. I am a scientist by necessity and not by vocation. I am really by nature an artist . . . and of this there lies an irrefutable proof: which is that in all countries into which psychoanalysis has penetrated it has been better understood and applied by writers and artists than by doctors. (pp. 130–134)

A significant component of our history as artists-therapists is suggested in this interview. It is apparent that Freud understood the central role that creativity and imagery played in his infant field of inquiry, psychoanalysis. It is important for the graduate student to be welcomed into the transformational process of graduate school and honored as one who is endeavoring to follow a rich tradition. This suggests an attitude of reverence on the part of the faculty members, supervisors, and mentors toward the student. Such an attitude is the marker for the student that the transformation has begun. To be held in high regard by one's teachers and mentors is often a new experience for the student, but it is crucial for all involved. For the student, being treated with respect is, in a sense, an initiation, a welcoming to the professional realm. For the faculty, mentor, or supervisor, responding to the student's undertaking with reverence is a reminder of the seriousness of the task. By revering the student, we guard against routinized interactions. Such an attitude by no means insures quality instruction, but it may increase the likelihood of success for the student.

The three threads of emphasis in this book—student, educator, practicing art therapist—are tightly interwoven in the fabric of our profession. It is absolutely clear to me that in order to do effective art therapy, one must possess passionate discipline. It is this quality that enables one to avoid the boredom of routine involvement. Whether in the role of teacher or student, supervisor or therapist, there can be no boredom if one stays in contact with the creative challenge of the work.

Each new student offers the teacher/supervisor myriad possibilities and obstacles. Each new client brings the therapist a mystery longing to be understood. Each new book, article, class, or interaction with a client presents the student with an invaluable opportunity to explore. This is the work that we do.

The client's ability to make the therapeutic journey is directly correlated with the passionate discipline of the therapist. The art therapist's passionate discipline is likewise proportionate to that of his or her teachers, mentors, and supervisors.

I close this chapter with a call to all in the field: *Attend to your passions.* If you have lost the zeal that once powered your journey, return to the studio, for it is there that you first stumbled upon the power of images and art processes. It is there that you can return when passions have cooled or discipline dissolved.

As I paint, I rediscover the work. I experience the struggle, the confusion, and the pain of artistic frustrations. Painting reminds me of my student years. Painting recalls the faces of clients I have known, and I hear the voices and questions of my students.

What does all this mean? What does all this mean?

This is the work of art therapy (Fig. 24).

Figure 24. As I paint, I rediscover the work

Chapter XII

THE YOUNG STUDENT

The Twelfth Essential–Being an art therapist demands a level of maturity and self-acceptance.

In this chapter, I will explore the particular strengths and struggles of students who have recently completed their undergraduate studies. As art therapy has become a more widely known and recognized discipline more and more students are entering graduate school immediately following undergraduate school. This is a positive sign that the art therapy profession is becoming an accepted discipline, but students who are younger and have less life experience present a particular set of challenges for educators.

Journal entry:

> Yesterday, my first day, was in some ways exciting and in other ways overwhelming. I realize how much I have to learn. By the time I arrived home last night I felt kind of numb. I had been bombarded by so many emotions I hardly felt anything. Just numbness. Then there are all the weird feelings of being the new kid on the block. Trying to come into a space that is new, not your own, and full of a zillion things that have been happening that you have no clue about. This morning as I listened to the reports about different clients and observed the people in the office, I wondered if they had some dichotomy between their personal and professional lives. I heard people talk about sharing feelings, being open and honest, developing good communication skills, etc., but were these things a part of their private lives? I don't know. I hope that I can learn for myself and others too . . . I have a lot of abbreviations to learn. I think I'll write down all the ones I don't know this afternoon at the meeting and then ask some people what they are.
>
> September, 1989
> Joan Selle

Becoming an art therapist is not an easy task. The doing of therapy demands a level of maturity and self-acceptance that is rare in the graduate student. It isn't their fault. In all likelihood it isn't anyone's fault. It's just the way things are.

In the summer of 1990, my wife Cathy and I went to a Tom Paxton concert in Columbus, Ohio. I was fascinated as I watched this well-known folk singer interact with the children in the audience. The concert was held outside in a park. The stage was set on top of a rise in the ground. Little kids ran up the hill, unimpressed by his list of musical accomplishments and unaware of the social conventions forbidding approaching a star. Their interest was in rolling down the hill, giggling, and wrestling with one another. I paid close attention, since my own kids were part of the chaos in front of Tom Paxton. I began to be embarrassed by their antics until I noticed the pleasure on the singer's face as he watched the rolling, tumbling, joyful scene before him. For a while he gave up singing his protest songs and social-consciousness ballads. Instead he offered *The Marvelous Toy, My Favorite Game,* and several other ditties suited to the children. He was neither offended nor distracted by the kids' engagement in life, but seemed to feed on their energy.

When a new cohort of students enter graduate school, it is easy for the seasoned art therapy professional to become irritated by their naiveté, their innocence, and their wide-eyed questioning about why things are the way they are. It is not unusual for graduate students to enter art therapy training programs directly after completion of their undergraduate degrees. Generally such students have not yet had a long-term relationship with a significant other, had children, suffered the loss of a job or lost loved ones through death. Vestiges of the adolescent's sense of immortality and idealism are blended with a deep yearning for a solidified sense of who they are. They bring energy, enthusiasm, and willingness to challenge the status quo. Many bring a lively and healthy curiosity, as well as an interest in soul-searching and introspection, but this is not always the case.

Recent undergraduates have been in a nearly constant state of transition for the past 10 years of life. They have gone from childhood through the rigors of adolescence and now find themselves on the front edge of responsible adulthood. In the best of circumstances, it has been a tough decade. Now they enter the world of graduate study to become therapists. There will be much reading to do, many papers to write, and numerous other academic hurdles. They will also be required to engage in unprecedented self-exploration, self-challenge, and honest self-evaluation. For many students, it is contrary to all of their personal experience.

My students remind me continually that things that are routine and commonplace for me (for instance, doing a drawing alongside my clients about a need that I have, or a feeling I experience) can be intensely threatening to a new student's sense of privacy. While students confront and learn to deal with questions of self-disclosure, I try to honor how hard this may be for them.

During practicum experiences a graduate student may face profound discomfort when joining an already-established art therapy group. While the other members of the group have had time to get to know one another, the student is introduced cold to the situation. If the group cultural norm is one of self-revelation and intimacy, the student may feel extreme internal pressure to conform. The result can be a disorienting sense of inadequacy, which often is expressed through devaluing or angry comments directed toward the educational program or the supervising ATR. It is essential that art therapy educators and supervisors respond with empathy to students' fears and pressures.

As Joan Selle recorded in her journal, the student quickly is made aware of how much there is to learn. This can be an overwhelming realization, and unless it is appropriately addressed, it can lead to destructive, self-defeating behavior by the student.

It is helpful for all new students, and particularly for younger students, in the first stages of the educational journey, to suggest the additional support of individual therapy. In the early stages of clinical work, students are exposed to forces they likely have never before encountered. Students are pushed toward personal growth and deepening by the unconscious motivations of others and disturbing client histories, mingled with intense daily interactions. It is helpful for faculty members and practicum supervisors to regularly remind students that the years they devote to graduate art therapy education may be some of the most difficult they will ever experience. The time can also be exciting and even fun, but personal therapy is recommended to enhance professional growth. I have often been aware, as a program director and supervisor, that students sometimes bring personal emotional material to supervisory sessions that would be better handled in a therapy session.

There are three areas of potential problems for the younger student in art therapy training environments. First, the struggle to define one-self as an adult may be problematic. If the student has gone directly from high school to undergraduate school and then to graduate study in art therapy, there has been little opportunity to function as an independent adult. The young person is soon placed in therapy situations, often with clients much older than the student. An internal refrain for the student may be, "How can I be therapeutic with this 40-year-old businessman? What do I know about the pressures and stress he has endured that led him to his depression?" These are valid and serious concerns for the student and must be addressed by the teacher/supervisor.

I remember how inept I felt as an art therapy student when a 52-year-old man wept in an art therapy session, sharing feelings about his impotence. What did I know of his experience? I was 23 years old. Oh, I knew what the word *impotence* meant, but the reality was so far removed from my experience that I was in no way able to be genuinely empathetic. Similarly, one of my students expressed her discomfort about her inability to respond to a woman suffering from postpartum depression. Although the student had researched the topic, she was still unable to grasp the depth of the mother's experience.

It is important for educators to be sensitive to the inadequacies of young students who lack experience. It is best for the supervisor to be looking for gaps in the student's knowledge and experience, and to have prepared an empathetic yet reality-based response.

Second, beyond developmental issues, there is the student's struggle to form a professional identity. It is not an easy transition to make from undergraduate student to art therapist-in-training. The focus must be shifted away from overconcern with grade-point averages and a sense that school is a series of vaguely relevant hoops to be jumped through. Instead, the focus is on the learning process as being integrally tied to the lives of others, i.e., future clients. This is a radical shift. To some degree, students also must get the message that the life's work of a healer is not simply an 8:00 to 5:00 occupation, but rather an approach to life. Being an art therapist is somewhat like being a physician or a minister—you are IT all the time.

Several years ago, one of my students learned a painful lesson. She attended a party given by one of her old college friends. In the midst of the evening, a former client, who had also been invited by a mutual acquaintance, approached her. They ended up sharing jokes with each other about various hospital staff, routines, and so forth. In this social situation, the student said some things that were inappropriate. Her comments would probably have been relatively harmless had not the former client been readmitted to the hospital a few weeks later. Their encounter at the party eventually came to light in an art therapy group and this undermined the student's authority and functioning in the group. This became destructive to the process of the group and eventuated in the student being removed from that particular group. The student was deeply embarrassed. It took quite some time to undo the damage to her self-esteem that the incident had caused.

An issue related to the development of professional identity is that of client confidentiality. It can be hard for some students to adhere to this requirement, but it is essential. When I was a student, one of my clients was part of a family with whom my sister was a friend. It was very difficult to deflect my sister's questions about the client. She did not understand the importance of my setting clear boundaries in relation to talking about the people I worked with at the hospital.

Another serious matter related to establishing professional boundaries is that of receiving gifts from clients. The young student often longs to be regarded as significant or important to the client. When I worked at the psychiatric hospital, my students and I struggled with this issue every Christmas. Invariably a client would purchase a gift for one of my students as a way to say, "Thank you for all you are doing." I had to tell the students that it was inappropriate to accept such gifts. It was painful for them to refuse the gifts, yet to accept them would be to change the nature of the relationship from therapeutic to that of friends.

One of my students entered a supervisory session appalled at a statement my colleague Deb DeBrular had made to a client. During a group feedback exercise, the client had said to Deb, "I think you are one of the best friends I've ever had." Deb's response was, "That's nice, but you need to know that I am not your friend." The student was angry with Deb for being, "so harsh and unfeeling." The task of the supervisory session became one of reframing for the student the nature of client/therapist relationships. It became an invaluable experience for the student as she wrestled with her own wishes to be accepted and liked by clients. It gave us an opportunity to work on the student's own evolving professional identity.

A third area of difficulty for all students, but particularly for younger students, is the process of exposing their vulnerabilities to clients by engaging in their own art work in the studio. This is an area of controversy within the profession at large. Some art therapists argue that the therapist should never draw or paint in the presence of the client. I take exception. I believe that such concerns are, at least in part, an outgrowth of a neo-Freudian position of blank-screen neutrality. Yet, art therapists have a role different from that of analysts. The art process calls for engagement, not aloof detachment. If the art therapist does not draw or paint, the range of interactive response to the client is unnecessarily limited to the verbal.

Of course, it is also true that the art therapist pays attention to *what* and *when* to share herself through personal art making. Her words are used only to verify the messages of the graphic images created by clients. That is to say, the communications of real consequence are *metaverbal.* Thus, art therapists' images are used in an intentional manner that facilitates the therapeutic interaction with clients. With education and experience, art therapy students develop sensitivity to what they are communicating to the client through the images they share.

I recall one student who was a participant in a girls' expressive group I led. Just before one group meeting, the student and I had been in a supervisory session. She had become angry with me, but we had not had time to bring our conflict to resolution. The task for each member of the group that day was to portray a feeling that each one had been struggling with. The student thought it would be inappropriate to depict her anger toward me, so she chose to do a drawing on the theme of emptiness. In fact, she decided to leave her paper blank, thinking that the vacant brown page was enough.

As others in the group worked on their drawings, I sensed the student's anger and resistance. In response, and perhaps as an expression of my anger at the student, I insisted that she draw something. She glared at me and then covered her entire page with light brown, almost the same color as the paper. As members of the group shared their work, the student remained silent. At one point, one of the adolescent girls said, "There's something weird in this group today." The client had picked up on the unspoken anger that had been passively expressed on the student's "empty" page and my insistence that she draw something.

For several months following this event, whenever the student and I met for supervision, I began each session with, "Well, let's talk about that day when you did not want to draw in expressive group." This set the stage for meaningful dialogue between us, revolving around issues of resistance, authority, conflict, and professional identity. It was no coincidence that during this same period, in the expressive therapy group, there were recurrent themes related to trust, vulnerability, and the expression of anger between adolescents and adults.

The struggles of the educational journey for younger students go hand-in-hand with the joys. These students often bring a level of enthusiasm, energy, and commitment that outweighs their naiveté and lack of experience and enables them to leap over the developmental hurdles.

As an art therapy educator and mentor, I am grateful for new students. They rekindle in me some of the wonder and awe I experienced as a novice art therapist when confronted with the power of art and the process of therapy. I recapture some of the way I felt after my first art therapy group. Through the students' struggles, I experience again the pain of my first disappointments and failures. Briefly, I revisit the old anger at institutional systems that often serve themselves more than the client. I am a comrade with my students as they run their idealistic heads into the walls of bureaucratic tradition.

Each time a new student intern enters the graduate program, I remind myself that there are priceless gifts the student offers and I celebrate the steady transfusion of lifeblood to the profession.

Chapter XIII

GIFTS OF THE FEMALE
AND MALE STUDENT

**The Thirteenth Essential–The differences between women
and men are as powerful and deep as one can imagine.**

In November, 1988, I participated in a weekend Tavistock group
relations training experience conducted by the A. K. Rice Institute
in Cincinnati. The Tavistock model is an intense, pressurized experience. As a colleague and I sat together waiting for the first session to
start, he commented on the sexual makeup of the group. There were
approximately seventy trainees, of whom five were men and sixty-five
were women. My colleague expressed some surprise and discomfort
that we were so clearly in the minority. I don't recall exactly how I
responded, but I do remember thinking, "So what else is new?"

As a male art therapist, I have been in the minority in my profession for the past 27 years. I remember feeling a little outnumbered
back in 1975 when I attended a meeting of the American Art Therapy
Association for the first time. Before that conference, every art therapist I had met was a man. My mentor was Don Jones, and many of the
stories I had heard were about men in the field. As I approached the
registration desk of the Galt Hotel in Louisville, Kentucky, I was
amazed to see so many women and so few men. At the time of this
writing, only six percent of the art therapists in the United States are
male (1998 AATA Membership Survey).

One of the dynamics that emerged in the Tavistock weekend
revolved around gender/political/power issues and sexual issues.
Because there were so few men in attendance, the group leader nick-
named the men, "the precious resource." I would posit that the same
is true within the art therapy profession. This is not to devalue the significant contributions of women to our field, but rather to acknowledge the need for balance in our discipline. The need for balance sug-

gests a parallel need for an awareness of and sensitivity to the special needs of male art therapists in graduate school (Fig. 25).

A Digression

For several years, I had the opportunity and pleasure to work as a co-therapist with Debra DeBrular in art therapy groups. One group was made up of six adolescent boys, aged 15 to 17, who suffered with severe emotional disturbances. As Deb and I worked to develop our co-leader relationship of this group, we explored our differences and how these affected the task of treating these difficult and resistive clients.

One day we introduced a symbolic group feedback exercise. Each member had drawn from a hat the name of another. The boys' task was to portray the person whose name they had drawn as some kind of plant, an animal and a machine.

Deb was always interested in how clients portrayed her. On that day she surveyed the completed drawings, wondering who had chosen her name. Her eyes fell on one page that held a drawing of a rose, a rabbit, and an oven.

This is what went through her mind:

> Oh, I thought, that one is me. Now, in no way do I see myself as being like a rabbit, a rose, or an oven. No, I would portray myself as perhaps like a gull, hunting above the sea, making nourishment of both the fresh fish and the garbage. Or like the hearty forsythia that blooms against the odds of the cold in the early spring. And comparing myself to a machine, I'd be an industrial sewing machine, rugged and sewing strong bonds.
>
> Still, I selected this picture of a rabbit, a rose and an oven as symbolic of myself. I was, after all, the only female member of that group. The other papers contained images of grizzly bears, army tanks, falcons, etc. Easily, no boy had characterized me in that way. I had been symbolized not as the flesh and blood person who lives in these clothes, but as the skirt.
>
> As Peter, the boy who had drawn the picture, explained his drawing to me, he said he saw me as warm, soft and pretty. I was unable to suppress my giggle at the irony of the situation. He had passed me by as a person, but still I believe he meant his portrayal of me as a compliment. While I might have preferred a more gutsy image of myself, I didn't really mind being thought of as warm or pretty.
>
> Aware of my thoughts and sharing a bit of my laughter, Bruce intervened, bringing to the group's collective mind a more realistic view of me. Ovens can burn, Bruce said. And adding a bit of drama, he acted out for them how my

Figure 25. The differences are as powerful and deep as one can imagine.

thorns had pricked him. Even Bruce didn't dare comment on the potential symbolism of the rabbit.

(Precious Gifts, 1989)

As our relationship developed, Deb and I became sensitive to images that seemed to reflect sexual stereotyping and gender-based developmental differences. Through many such encounters I began to be more sensitive to the unique patterns and metaphors of growth that my maleness has fostered. Gender-based developmental differences are powerful and deep and may have contributed to conflicts between women and men over power and prestige for a long time. We must begin to address them not as battlefields but as potential gifts that we men and women arts therapists have to offer one another.

To understand the peculiar predicament of men in the art therapy profession, it will be helpful to explore the developmental differences between men and women. In order to explore some traditional themes in masculine development, Nelson (1985) begins his article with a brief passage from Allan Sillitoe's (1959) *The Loneliness of the Long Distance Runner:*

> All I knew was that you had to run, run, run, without knowing why you were running, but on you went, through fields that you didn't understand and into woods that made you afraid, over hills without knowing you'd been up and down, and shooting across streams that would have cut the heart out of you had you fallen into them. And the winning post was no end to it, even though the crowds might be cheering you in, because on you had to go. (Sillitoe, 1959, pp. 37–38)

In Sillitoe's portrait of the runner, we are presented with an image of loneliness, strenuous performance, competition, and uncertainty about the point of it all. These are poignant themes that many men confront daily in their lives. From early childhood, men are taught the worth of individual accomplishment, mastery, and the joy of beating one's opponent.

In the years that I worked with female co-therapists, I have spent much energy trying to understand my developmental experience as a male. In doing so, I have come to grips with what I bring to a group, to co-therapy relationships, and to teaching encounters with predominantly female students.

Parallels have been drawn between the masculine body and the recurrent metaphoric themes it generates. Nelson (1985) proposes that, "Without intending a biological determinism, we can still acknowledge that the male biological experience encourages certain tendencies different from those commonly experienced by women" (p. 1).

Nelson goes on to delineate some of the body metaphors:

> Male genitals are external, visible and easily accessible to touch . . . generating a greater tendency to focus and reinforce male sexual feelings in the genitals. Also, particularly in adolescence, the male experiences erections at awkward times and in unwanted situations, an experience which tends to persuade him that the penis is beyond voluntary control. (p. 1)

Nelson (1985) suggests that these bodily experiences seem to incline men toward certain spiritual forms. One is externality. Mystery is not within, but rather out there. Mystery is to be penetrated by a self that is defined by specific boundaries. Generally, the masculine accent upon act and performance is significantly different from the feminine emphasis on relationship and meaning. From the male perspective, sexual experience is focused in an act during which they must perform, whereas women tend to experience their sexuality as a mysterious internal process.

When I was four or five years old I was given a basketball for my birthday. A bushel basket was nailed to a door in our basement. I quickly learned that there was much praise and recognition to be gathered by my hours of practicing alone. I was credited with being a very good boy when I learned to dribble with both hands. I recall few such rewards for my developing relating skills. By the time I was seven, I was sure that a man had to do the important things by himself, and that if I practiced I could learn to perform the actions skillfully (Fig. 26).

Another masculine body metaphor stems from the physical position of the testicles. This most vulnerable part of the male body is hidden away, tucked behind the penis and between the legs. The bio-metaphoric message is: *protect your vulnerability, keep it hidden.* This is paradoxical, of course. In order for the testicles to do what they are designed to do, i.e., make sperm, they must hang loose, away from the body, in order to maintain the correct temperature. The paradox is that while men must protect and hide their vulnerability, if they want to participate in the most profoundly intimate creative act, men must be vulnerable.

In addition, the musculature of the male lends itself to visions of domination, overpowering force and defeat of the other. Such images give insight of the roots of the difficulties men often have with intimacy. For many men there is comfort in expression of the competitive drive, discomfort in being close to someone else. In myriad social encounters during their early years, men are presented with the messages: big boys don't cry; there's nothing to be afraid of; you have to take care of things yourself to be a man. Men are comfortable patting one another on the back, or arm wrestling, or banging into one another on the court or playing field. Men are often uncomfortable hugging, or disclosing to our male friends how meaningful thy find their friendships.

Chowdorow (1978) observed that, "mothers experience their sons as their male opposite." To define their own identity, boys begin early to separate themselves physically from their mothers. Male development has a clearly defined individuation process. Being called a *momma's boy*

Figure 26. By the time I was seven, I was sure that a man had to do the important things by himself.

by young male peers is commonly understood to be a slur, challenging a boy's masculinity.

As a male art therapist and teacher I bring to clinical and educational settings my personal experiences of externalization. I bring a deep ingrained belief that my worth is measured by how I perform, how well I have mastered the world. I bring a core belief that vulnerability and intimacy must be approached with great caution. These innate beliefs sometimes cause conflict in my relationships with women students. Sometimes we complement each other. Likewise, in clinical work, male art therapists will at times experience distance from their clients because of their masculine traits.

To some degree, male art therapy students bring each of these aspects of self to the graduate school environment. At times, these masculine aspects can be problematic and at other times they can be strengths. There are occasions when the male student must overcome obstacles that have their roots in his masculinity. Even so, I believe that men who are art therapists are a valuable resource for our profession.

To contrast the male developmental experience with that of women, I begin with some words from my colleague, Deb DeBrular. We co-authored a paper for presentation at the 1989 national conference of the American Art Therapy Association, held in San Francisco. Here are some of her words:

> When I was twenty-three and pregnant for the first time, I hoped and prayed for a boy. Everyone knew I wanted a boy and my parents hoped along with me. They probably had secret concerns that if my baby turned out to be a girl, I would be disappointed. I wanted a boy, not because of any culturally dictated social order about having a boy first and a girl second; not because of any illusions about creating the perfect family. I wanted a boy because, having grown up as a girl myself, I couldn't see what our culture offered a girl that would make it so nice.
>
> Where I grew up women were seen either as marriage material or sex objects. Being a sex object was bad and offered a future of repeatedly being used by guys who only wanted one thing. Being marriage material was good and offered respect and financial security. If a girl made the decision to be marriage material, she guarded fiercely her reputation. One venture into erotic behavior could cast her into the role of the sex object, never to return. The journey into eroticism could take various routes. She could lose her head in the back of Joe's dad's car, leaving herself subject to the whims of Joe's advances. Or, the erotic, sexual event could be done against her will. Either way, secrecy was a must.
>
> Wanting the best for their daughter, my parents molded me into marriage

material. The script called for secretarial courses in high school, a secretarial job until marriage, then marriage to the right man who would provide for our children and me. Working for a few years before the kids arrived would be tolerated, but no self-respecting man would allow his wife to work, and so after marriage, I would stay at home. My deviations from the script are another story, but at twenty-three and pregnant, life seemed pretty grim.

When I was thirty-five and pregnant again, I wanted a daughter more than anything else in the world. Where years earlier I could define why I had not wanted a daughter, now I wanted one because of some deep, undefinable feeling. My daughter's arrival was met with joy, but also some sobering thoughtfulness on my part. Here in this precious bundle was a feminine creature that would have me as her role model. I, who hadn't really valued being feminine myself. I had a dilemma. If I could not value being feminine, couldn't value myself, then surely I could not value this tiny female creature. The shock sent me exploring what it meant to be feminine. The exploring led to my profound belief that research being done on the feminine experience is important work that, if not ignored, if we do take notice, will impact every area of our work.

Bruce and I, by virtue of our opposite genders, bring very different things into a relationship, into our therapy groups. What we bring individually has universal qualities. Describing, listing and naming these qualities can possibly be done best by first looking at biology. Our bodies are our first presentations to the world, determining how others will treat us and how we will learn to behave.

What does it mean to be feminine? On the birthing table, the doctor looks to the genitals to determine gender. It is by the hidden nature of the female organs that the doctor and the parents know a little girl has been born. Who can deny the importance of gender when we look at how this first noticed characteristic determines so much of what the child's life will be?

Traditionally, developmental theory has not taken into account the experience of little girls. Male experience has been studied with the assumption that girls do something similar, or as Freud would have it, some strange contorted mirror-image of male developmental theory. More recently, work by Nancy Chowdorow (1978), Carol Gilligan (1982), Jean Baker Miller (1987), Judith Jordan (1986), and others present the theory that the process of development for girls is very different. Girls are more often raised by primary caretakers of the same sex. The mother and her daughter share the common characteristics of hidden genitals. The daughter comes to know herself as feminine, not through visible evidence, but through the common experience of having something hidden within the body. A mother experiences her daughter as more like herself. Her relationship with the daughter is characterized by attachment.

Little girls come to relate from this experience of attachment and sharing of hiddenness. Several years ago, I heard a presentation by Jean Baker Miller in which she used the image of an elementary school playground. What are the children doing? The boys are involved in active, competitive games, and the girls are gathered in knots with their best friends, sharing secrets about their relationships.

No little girl in our culture escapes having witnessed thousands of pictures of women scantily dressed, the camera accenting the curves of their figures. It was for this reason that I commented to Bruce early in writing our paper that this was a greater risk for him than for me. Women are accustomed to seeing the female body displayed, but for men to be so exposed is less common. Nudity and exposure are symbols, metaphors, for vulnerability. Part of being a woman is being vulnerable. Not only are we exposed, we are physically smaller. Not only are we portrayed as victims by movies and television, we actually are often victimized in the real world.

When a girl reaches the age of twelve or so, she begins to see physical evidence of her femininity in the reality of her changing body. Biologically, the purpose of the changes that take place in the female body is to provide life to another. The woman's shape becomes the nest, breasts give nourishment. Marie, one of our fourteen-year-old patients, said she believes women must need a softer body because, 'they grow babies inside of themselves.' The metaphorical theme is one of giving and providing, yet it is a struggle to reconcile the biological purpose with the cultural message.

For women, the sexual act itself has a passive quality. A woman may choose to take an active role in a sexual relationship, but it is not necessary for either reproduction or for bringing satisfaction to her sexual partner. One interpretation of this phenomenon points to the less competitive nature of women, that assurance of their feminine role is not dependent on performance. Having less anxiety surrounding our sexual role, women are able to place more importance on *being*, in that they have less to prove.

Still, anxiety does exist around the feminine metaphor of sexual intercourse. It is, however, a different metaphor from the male. At Harding Hospital, part of my job was using art processes to assess children and adolescents coming into the acute unit, which opened in 1989. As I observed the issues the young girls brought to the assessment process, one theme recurred. It was concern about intrusion. The girls seemed to be asking, *Will I experience what you do to me as intrusion?*

Many of the girls I saw had been sexually abused, but they are not the only ones who expressed this fear. When I think of the fear of intrusion in light of gender issues and the metaphor of the feminine experience of sexual intercourse, it makes perfect sense.

This is not to say that all sexual intercourse is experienced as an intrusion, but certainly women are always aware of the possibility. While writing this paper, I encouraged Bruce to consider the almost exclusively male act–rape–as one aspect of his presentation. As we talked and processed, it was clearly a struggle for Bruce to think about what to say about rape, about the link between sex, violence and rage. I became frustrated. What I finally realized was that I have thought a lot more about rape than Bruce has. I suspect that women think about rape a lot more than men do.

In considering what I think I saw in my art therapy assessments with young girls—a fear of intrusion—I became aware of how that fear played a part in my negotiating a co-therapy relationship with Bruce. The question has not been the overt, *would Bruce rape me?* but rather the more metaphorical, *would he leave me to be myself? Can I maintain myself in his company?* I suspect I made Bruce feel uncomfortable and on-the-spot more than once over this issue. Not that I ever concretely expressed this fear of intrusion. I leaked enough metaphors, however, that at one point in our pre-group processing, Bruce said to me, "Deb, I will not sexually abuse you." Although at the time this seemed, even to me, a strange thing for him to say, I now believe that sexual abuse is a metaphor for the more subtle, subliminal devaluing of women that happens in our culture.

As a woman I bring this concern about intrusion to the therapeutic process. I bring the feminine history of being devalued and undervalued, and the historical feminine experience of adapting to the subordinate role. I bring my less competitive nature and my comfort with simply *being*. I bring my protection and my nurturance. I bring my desire for strong attachments and my need for relationships to have meaning. All of these aspects of myself can be experienced as problems or as strengths. In honoring our differences, Bruce and I strove to allow them to be strengths.

To illustrate the impact of our developmental differences, our efforts to deal with them in our relationship and the effect this has upon art therapy groups, I share a few brief clinical vignettes:

As we walked into the small expressive arts therapy room that morning, the atmosphere was charged with hostile energy. The five adolescent boys, 15 to 17 years of age, had just come from a turbulent community meeting on their unit. During the course of that meeting, several of the nurses had been confronting two of our group members for a variety of aggressive, obnoxious, and disrespectful behaviors on the unit. Mumbled epithets cut through the air, "Those fucking bitches" . . . "I'd like to stick something up her ass. . . ." and so on.

The drawing task my co-therapist Deb and I had decided upon for the session was, "Cover your page in red and brown, then imagine that it is a section of your own brick wall. What, if any, graffiti would be on the wall?" The boys worked fiercely and the air was heavy with red-brown chalk dust. What emerged graphically were powerful images of rage, expressed in hostile, aggressive, sexualized slogans. Among these: "You are a cocksucker" . . . "Fuck you, cunt" . . . "On the rag" . . . "Eat me, bitch" . . . and the like.

As I turned from my own graffiti and looked at the clients' work, I braced myself for wrestling with the anger and rage that was presented. I looked at Deb's drawing. The contrast was striking. I saw her wall, but I also saw a fragile vine growing up the bricks. For a moment, seeing this small, green life, I was furious with the clients in the group. Inside my head I screamed, *How dare you jerks speak and draw in such a filthy way with Deb in the room?* I was tempted to assume a gallant stance and defend this poor frail vine from the vile creatures that surrounded her. My internal dialogue continued, *To hell with how these kids feel. I have to protect Deb! I have to step in and control . . . even conquer them!* An indignant, self-righteous inner voice exclaimed, *Surely I have never treated a woman so crudely, surely I know how to behave (or perform) properly with women . . . I've never, ever . . .* and then the inner voice said, *If only Deb weren't here. I know exactly how I'd handle this if it was just us guys in the room.*

In a matter of seconds, all my old tapes about externalizing and performing and solo activity had played within me. I took an emotional step backward and said out loud to the group, "Wow, there is a lot of feeling on the walls today."

Deb said, "I would like to start us off by sharing what I've drawn."

She began by talking about her wall as being something that protects, but also inhibits her. She continued her description by saying, ". . . and I think this vine is about my being a woman. Today I'm really aware that I am the only woman in the group. It seems dangerous in here today." The boys quickly attempted to disavow that their drawings had anything to do with Deb. "It's just those bitches on the unit."

But Deb would not let up. She said, "I hear you say that, but still I see all these angry and sexualized images and I know that women have often been victimized by men. What you do affects me deeply."

The rest of the session was spent in disentangling the violence and sexualized aggression that had been cast on the walls. Several times the group looked to me as if to say, *Explain this to her . . . please.* I resisted the temptation to say, "Aw, come on, Deb, this is just the way guys talk. Don't personalize this." It would have given permission to their behavior.

I believe that each of the boys walked out of that group room on that day with a different sense of male/female relationships for having experienced Deb's vulnerability and my refusal to rationalize their behavior. I could not have brought about that result by myself.

On another occasion, Jan, a woman in her forties, was a relatively new member of our art therapy student group, but already her presence was having a curious effect. Clearly, Jan had some issues with me. As weeks passed, Deb and I observed Jan's increasing demand for my attention. She did not seek my approval, or appear needy in any way. No, Jan wanted to fight with me. She was always finding new ways to debate with me.

"Why do you want to fight with me?" I would ask. Jan didn't know, but clearly she loved to hate me. At the same time it was evident that Deb didn't matter to Jan . . . Deb was a non-entity.

Outside of the group, the students buzzed about Jan's behavior towards me. Their conversations and concerns were leaked to Deb and me in various ways as the students struggled with the intensity of their feelings of competitiveness and anger. It was especially difficult for new members of the student group who were trying to understand the dynamics of group process and could not figure out the divisive atmosphere.

During group sessions, images that were perhaps symbolic of masculinity began to appear more frequently in drawings, most depicted in the context of dangerous situations. One woman drew herself slaying a great, half-hidden sea dragon. At first we regarded these images as the emergence of issues about men. Later, Deb suggested they might pertain more to the group's discomfort with Jan's hostility towards me.

When the conflict was at its peak, Deb and I asked the group to draw how they saw us as leaders of the group. Sharing her drawing, Jan said that she disliked my style; I was too confrontive for her taste, too directive and strong.

When it was Deb's turn to share, she began, "I think my presence is essential in this group right now." She went on to explain to the students that she knew how to have a relationship with me. "I don't want to change him," she said. "In fact, I like him just fine the way he is. Bruce can be at times very much like the thunderstorm, like the lightening that cracks and makes us shiver. I think I am essential to this group because I know how to have what everyone else in the group seems to want, a relationship with Bruce. I am that comforting assurance at the end of the long road through the dark, stormy night."

Deb's intervention seemed to take some of the fire out of Jan. In later group sessions Jan was able to focus her energies on issues other than fighting with me. Perhaps the more important result of Deb's intervention was the relief of the rest of the group when Deb contained Jan. They understood perfectly. She had modeled how one woman stays intact in a thunderstorm.

With these vignettes as background, I will explain the process of exploring our relationship in the groups we led. At one time we had three groups: a group of male adolescents; a female adolescent group, and the student art therapy training group. The adolescent clients brought a swirl of complex emotions and behaviors. The students brought their anxieties, excitement and issues of gender and authority. In different ways, each group challenged our relationship. There were attempts to split us, devour us, idealize, devalue and destroy us.

Deb and I often talked of our relationship as the vessel that contained the group's affect and emotion. I thought of a container made of clay, molded and fired, glazed and strengthened by time (Fig. 27).

Deb imaged a woven basket, a vessel that was flexible and pliant, capable of changing shape with the ebb and flow of group currents.

One image that we agreed upon was the image of what lay between us as we met in pre- and post-group discussion. Between us lay an imaginary basket, filled with bits of fabric, nuts and bolts, crumpled paper, and shards of glass. One of us would pick up some scrap that seemed important. We examined it, got the feel of it, sometimes holding it close and sometimes discarding it as meaningless. These symbolic bits and pieces of past experience were the makings of our relationship. They represented feelings ranging from deep mutual respect to irritation; from warm friendship to disappointment; from laughter to scowls; from tears to silences. Some were bits of history; some were pieces of the present. We attended to them and, in so doing, we attended to the members of the groups we led.

One of our earliest experiences with this basket image happened about six months after we'd begun working as a co-therapy team. We had known each other for six or seven years and felt that our relationship work had already been done. We were mistaken. The adolescent boys' group was focusing on how guys treat girls. Confronted by Deb, one of the boys turned to me and challenged, "So what makes you 'n' hers thing such hot shit?"

We resisted the client's attempt to place us in the role of subjects in the group, but after group we agreed to spend our next supervision session talking specifically about our relationship. Our discussion led us back to our early days, traveled past old hurt feelings and anger, covering our basic admiration of each other and our enjoyment of each other as friends. It was not an easy hour. The self-disclosure

Figure 27. A container made of clay.

seemed endless.

During the very next session of the boys' group, the same client who had challenged us raised again the issue of relationships. Deb and I were more prepared. This time, the concern floating about the room was not how boys treat girls; it was about how the boys in the group were treating one another. What began as angry confrontation between two relationship-shy, acting-out macho boys evolved into choked-back tears, drawings of hearts, expressions of feelings for each other and even words of love. I have no doubt that this was the first time in either boy's life he had risked such exposure. Deb and I felt honored to witness the moment.

Such work in the group could not have been done without the work Deb and I did in our relationship. Although no mention of it was made in the group, our work together provided an environment of safety that was beyond words.

Despite our conscious efforts to acknowledge our developmental differences and honor them, we sometimes failed to attend to each other. Sometimes I acted oppressively; some days I felt manipulated by Deb's passivity. We'd pull something out of the basket that cut or battered us, and for a while we'd bleed and cover our bruises.

Although we worked hard at our relationship, it was not a perfect co-therapy team. But we did work.

Our exploration of gender issues strongly affected our art therapy student group. As young men and women trying to define themselves in relation to their world, our students ran into their own biases and barriers. By being sensitive to the topic, by keeping actively aware of the gender issues between ourselves, we did not neglect, gloss over, or bury them at the bottom of our basket. We provided for the group a container where it was safe for gender issues to be acknowledged and addressed.

The art therapy profession will likely remain predominantly female for some time to come. It is essential that faculty members and supervisors in graduate programs be sensitive to the unique gifts brought by both female and male students. Men and women approach the task of learning differently. Female students may come bearing an innate awareness of the value of relationships, intimacy, and vulnerability. Male students may bring an appreciation for mastery of technique, skillful performance, and individual accomplishment. These different, developmentally-grounded approaches have much to offer one other. It is essential, for the health and richness of our discipline, that educational programs be aware of and appreciative of these differences. The creative arts therapies may provide an atmosphere that honors the polarities of masculinity and femininity as precious gifts.

Chapter XIV

THE ROLE OF PHILOSOPHY

The Fourteenth Essential–A philosophy must be present in order for coherent, consistent art therapy to occur.

> *philosophic, adj. pertaining to philosophy;*
> *calm, wise and thoughtful.*
> *philosophize, v. to reason like a philosopher.*
> *philosopher, n. one noted for calm judgment and*
> *practical wisdom.*
> *philosophy, n. study of the causes and relations*
> *of things and ideas; the serene wisdom that comes*
> *from calm contemplation of life and the universe.*
> Teall, E. N. (Ed.). New Concise Webster's Dictionary, p. 227.

By this point it is no doubt clear that I am much less concerned with instructing students (or sharing with colleagues) creative arts therapy methods or techniques than I am with discussing philosophies of why we do what we do. Specific creative arts techniques and methodologies must be born and evolve within the contexts of individual therapists and their particular clinical settings. This is not to say that the session structures I employ in my work with clients and students would not apply to other program settings. My intent is to stress the need for a clear and articulate philosophy of treatment within each and every individual art therapist, regardless of location. I do not imply that *my philosophy* must be adhered to, but that *a philosophy* must be present in order for coherent, consistent arts therapy to occur.

In a broader sense, this same maxim can and should be applied to clinical settings and systems as well. According to a psychiatrist and former colleague of mine, Dr. Robert Huestis, "Anything [within reason] that all of the caregivers on a given treatment unit agree is beneficial to the client will be beneficial to the client" (Huestis, R. personal communication, 1996).

108

In 27 years of clinical art therapy work, I have been on the staff of two sorts of treatment programs: those that had a unified and agreed-upon treatment philosophy, and those in which significant segments of the treatment team were at odds with one another. The relative merits of the two were dramatically evidenced in the progress made by clients. In my experience, it seemed that when treatment programs had a clear philosophy, clients tended to progress well. When a program's philosophic approach was unclear, clients often suffered as a result.

A philosophy of treatment is effective only if its intellectual constructs about the nature of therapy for a given emotional or physical illness are successfully applied at a practical level. An example of Dr. Huestis' viewpoint as it relates to an inpatient psychiatric treatment program, might be as follows:

If all members of a treating staff working with emotionally disturbed adolescents agreed it was important for each client to start the treatment day with an outdoors morning walk at 7:30 a.m., I believe that (1) this would happen in spite of the resistance one might expect from clients, and (2) that it would in fact be a therapeutic element in the lives of individual clients. I cite this example purposely because it may at first glance appear trivial and mundane. Yet, when all caregivers understand the philosophic grounding of such a structure, it will likely be of benefit.

The philosophic underpinnings behind a 7:30 a.m. constitutional hike could be grounded in an awareness of the nature of psychiatric illness and strategies for recovery:

A. During sleep, many people experiencing depression seem to have less oxygen going to the brain, exacerbating the depression. It is well known that morning is one of the most difficult periods of the day for the depressed individual. Physical exercise seems to be beneficial because it increases the flow of oxygen to the brain.

B. Persons suffering with psychiatric disorders often enter treatment programs when their lives are in varying degrees of chaos. The predictable structure of a daily morning walk could be a potent meta-message about the need for routine in one's life.

C. Consistent, external structure is an unspoken metaphor that can be internalized, building and strengthening intrapsychic structure.

D. For the person with symptoms of schizophrenia, the establishment of a daily regimen of routine actions forms the foundation of reality orientation.

E. Shared communal tasks establish identification with the notion that therapy is a consistent process that must be worked on daily.

F. For the adolescent struggling with a conduct disorder, a morning walk would set the stage for a treatment day filled with clear, consistent expectations and the establishment of a safe, predictable environment.

I could discuss at greater length the philosophy behind a 7:30 a.m. walk, but the five points serve as examples of underlying reasons for such a structure. For art therapists, there are certainly parallels between this example and art processes. For example, it is important for an art therapist to understand the underlying reasons for engaging a person with a thought disorder in art processes that reinforce reality orientation, such as repetitive motor tasks. Likewise, it is important that an art therapist be clear about the potential therapeutic benefits for an impulsive adolescent boy who prepares his own canvas for painting, rather than buying a pre-stretched, pre-gessoed canvas.

One's philosophic approach to art therapy–that is, the thoughtful framework that provides the underpinnings for the myriad details of one's work–enables the art therapist move freely within well-established therapeutic parameters. Having a clear philosophy of art therapy protects the integrity of the therapy and assures the client that the therapist is not operating out of a *whatever works* or *fly by the seat of the pants* approach.

As an existential art therapist, my philosophical basis leads me to build my role around three tenets: (1) I do with (and be with) my clients, right where they are, just as they are; (2) I am open and attentive to my clients' lives and in turn open my life to them; and perhaps most important, (3) I bring an attitude of respect and honor to my clients' pain (Moon 1995). By doing these three things, I engage clients in a process of transformation that helps them shift from the position of victim to that of hero. The art therapy process is a journey. I go along as a fellow pilgrim. I offer a story as illustration:

Lori was admitted to the short-term child and adolescent unit through the psychiatric emergency service. She was 14 years old, from a small college town in southern Ohio. On the night before her admission to the hospital she had attempted suicide by ingesting an overdose of amphetamines and alcohol.

She had a distinctive style about her. She wore jeans with multiple suggestive tears, a bright red headband and painted black Nikes. She introduced herself as a "skater-hood" who was part of a skate gang. Her first reference to me was in the form of a derisive comment to a peer as I was walking through the unit, "So who's the bald dude?"

On her first day in the art therapy group I co-led with Dr. Carol Lebeiko, Lori told us in no uncertain terms how she felt about being in the hospital. "I don't need to be in this fucking place and I am not about to be in no treatment."

I responded, "Well, Lori, you're in good company. Look around yourself. No one in this group wants to be in a psychiatric hospital. This is not anybody's idea of an ideal vacation resort."

Dr. Lebeiko then gave her standard introduction to the group. "Lori, this is a group where we use drawings as a way to get in touch with and share feeings."

Lori snapped, "I can't draw and I don't have any feelings."

Carol continued, "You don't have to be a great artist. Whatever you do will be accepted here. But, we do ask that whatever is said in here must stay in here. That way it is safe. We begin and end every session by checking in with how people are feeling."

With that said we began our opening ritual. I asked the group members to imagine themselves as some kind of a landscape. "Knowing the kind of person you are, the kind of life you've had, what sort of a landscape would you be? Draw the landscape that is you."

Dr. Lebeiko and I, along with the five clients other than Lori, stood, gathered chalk and moved to one of the large pieces of paper taped to the wall and began to draw.

Lori sat, glaring defiantly. "I can't draw and I don't want to do this crap."

Carol picked up a box of chalk and gently placed it upon Lori's lap. She said, "Just trust your hand, Lori. Whatever you make will be okay."

After a few minutes Lori went to stand in front of a piece of paper and began to draw. The image that emerged was of a vast and empty field, a small clump of weeds in the lower right corner, and a stormy night sky.

When everyone had finished drawing we sat back in our circle of chairs and began to tell stories about the landscapes on the walls. As one boy spoke of his raging sea, I noticed Lori talking and laughing under her breath to the girl sitting next to her. I interrupted the boy's story, "Brian, how does it make you feel to have Lori and Amy talking while you are sharing your drawing?"

Brian's face reddened, he looked down at the floor and shyly replied,

"Oh, it's okay. I don't really mind."

I put my hand to my head and exclaimed, "But Brian, you should mind. It's not okay, not okay at all."

Lori reacted, "You don't really expect us to take this shit serious, do you?" She laughed.

"Lori, one thing I know about everybody in this group is that you all have a long history of people not taking your feelings seriously. In this group, Dr. Lebeiko and I promise always to pay attention."

Lori groaned, "Give me a break. These are just stupid pictures. They don't mean a thing."

Carol said, "Bruce and I believe that everything we create is a self-portrait. We take it very seriously."

The group was very quiet. Lori looked around for some support for her resistance, but found none. After a few moments of silence, I suggested we return to Brian's sea.

When it came time to hear about Lori's desolate and stormy landscape, she said, "I still don't think this means anything."

I said, "Yowsa, I am fascinated by this place you have drawn. I can almost hear the wind . . . feel it on my face."

Lori sneered, "Be careful you don't get blown away."

I responded, "Oh Lori, I've been in lots of stormy places. I'm interested in yours, but not afraid of it."

Carol said, "It must be hard on those plants in the corner."

"They're just weeds." Lori said.

Carol replied, "They look like they could be blown away."

Lori, looking at her drawing said, "Maybe they should be. They're just trash."

Melanie, a girl who had been in the group for a few sessions asked, "Do you ever feel that way, Lori? I mean that's a little like how you said your dad makes you feel."

That was all it took. Lori's tough bravado crumbled. Tears welled up in her eyes. She looked away. The group was magnificently quiet.

"It's okay, Lori, you don't have to say anything more. I think everyone in the group has heard you. We understand. We believe you," I said.

Lori was in the group for another three weeks, six sessions all-together. During that time the walls were covered with scenes of her loneliness, brought on by her mother who had abandoned the family years before. Fires of rage burned as Lori depicted her father's alcoholism and abuse of her. Lori, perhaps for the first time in her life, experienced the deep relief of being understood and taken seriously by adults. Carol and I attended to and honored the deep pain and self-loathing Lori felt upon admission. The pain eased and the loathing lightened.

During her hospitalization Lori mustered the courage to confront her father. She implored him to seek treatment for his alcoholism. As fate would have it, he complied and at last report their lives were going much better, one day at a time. Lori's suffering found meaning. As she put it, "If I hadn't tried to kill myself, my dad and I couldn't live together." Lori's last drawing portrayed her weeds transformed into a rose bush. There were plenty of flowers, and a healthy dose of sharp thorns as well.

The basic tenets of existentialism are that pain, frustration, guilt, loss, loneliness, and anxiety, all aspects of human anguish, are unavoidable for human beings. Existential writers are skeptical of materialism and hedonism. Recurrent themes in existentialist literature are that struggle, suffering, and anguish are not only inescapable, but that the individual's efforts to cope with them form the basis of an authentic, full, and potentially noble existence.

As an art therapist, I am well acquainted with the anguish, suffering and struggle of my clients. As an existentialist, I am equally familiar with my own inner turmoil. This is the historic dwelling place of the artist and the figurative home of many suffering and disturbed people I've treated.

An existential philosophical base, integrated with my background in the arts and professional experience as an art therapist, gives me a solid and consistent perspective in treating my clients. Throughout time the artists of the world—painters, dancers, playwrights, poets—have abandoned the pursuit of monetary success and material comfort in their quest for values and truths that go to the depths of human existence. It has always been the artists of a culture who seek the meaning of life.

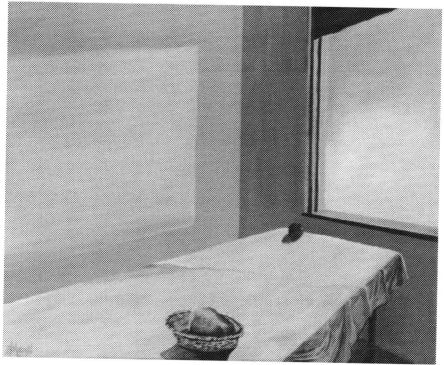

Figure 28. Truths that go to the depths of human existence.

An existential philosophical base offers an opportunity to be with clients in the midst of their anguish, not for the purpose of making the anguish go away, but in an effort to find the meaning of their pain and bring a sense of honor to their circumstance.

A Philosophy of Teamwork: Integration Versus Exclusion

A prominent area of concern within the creative arts therapy professions is that the arts therapist must be a competent team member and be able to maintain a professional and competent identity as a therapist" (Dulicai, Hays & Nolan, 1989). I want to briefly examine the phrase "team member," for this relates directly to the subject of treatment philosophy.

Many art therapy positions operate within a multi-disciplinary team context. It is imperative that educational programs prepare students for this rewarding and challenging professional milieu. This requires helping students develop a sense of professional identity that is grounded in a coherent philosophy of art therapy. Unfortunately, students are not always prepared to work in collegial collaboration with professionals from other disciplines. "Current mental health clinical practice requires a level of sophistication beyond the technician-oriented activities therapist model" (Dulicai, Hays & Nolan, 1989, pp. 11–14). This seems to suggest a subtle devaluation of activity-oriented disciplines that does nothing to elevate the art therapy profession. As art therapists, we need not compete with psychiatrists, social workers, nurses, counselors, occupational therapists, horticulture therapists, and psychologists. Maneuvers that seek to portray art therapy as better than another profession are ultimately self-defeating. Making art is an integrating process that thrives on the value of divergent materials and flourishes on the respectful incorporation of different perspectives. I am deeply appreciative of the lessons I have learned from occupational therapists, recreation therapists, and activity-oriented therapists. Members of these disciplines and more have taught me the value of the sophisticated therapy that happens in the greenhouse, the crafts shop, and on the basketball court. Their lessons are every bit as valuable as those garnered from psychiatrists, psychologists, and social workers. After all, the aim of all these disciplines is to help clients to ease their pain.

Many of my art therapy colleagues over the years have objected to being referred to as *adjunctive therapists*. I would argue that if there is a genuine team treatment approach to clinical work, all members of the team are adjunct to one another. The physician is adjunct to the social worker, who is adjunct to the art therapist, who is adjunct to the recreation therapist, etc., etc.

In graduate-level art therapy educational programs we have a responsibility to prepare art therapists who are skilled in performing their clinical tasks and also skilled in communicating and collaborating with doctors, nurses, psychologists, and social workers. We emphasize the importance of teamwork in which one discipline is not in competition with another, but rather in concert with them. In team sports, it is essential that all members of a team work together toward their goals. In therapy, it is likewise necessary that each member of the team work collaboratively with colleagues toward the end of restoring emotional or mental health to the client.

Art therapy educators can begin to lay the groundwork for authentic cooperation by refraining from making devaluing references to other disciplines and keeping in mind the integrative quality of the arts processes. By doing so we can counteract the disciplinary pretentiousness that sometimes infects professions.

Art therapy educators can strive to provide students with a sense of professional identity and self-confidence based upon the unique gifts that arts therapists bring to clinical settings. This strong sense of identity is best conveyed through the role modeling of professors, mentors, and supervisors. The role model can give the student an image of positive professionalism that acknowledges and respects the contributions of a wide variety of therapy disciplines.

Art therapists who work from a clearly articulated philosophy, whatever its perspective, have a framework for understanding, coping with, and treating clients. Graduate art therapy educational programs and clinical treatment programs that make serious, intentional efforts to develop and communicate their philosophy provide a service to students in the field as well as to the clients who are served. As Nietzsche said, "He who has a *why* to live for can bear almost any *how*" (Frankl, 1959, p. 97). To paraphrase Nietzsche for this context, I would say, "She who has calmly thought through why she does what she does will surely understand how to do it wisely."

Chapter XV

THERAPY AND HOLIDAYS

The Fifteenth Essential–The work of art therapy takes no vacations.

An area of consideration that has received little attention in our literature in relation to art therapists is the effect of significant holidays on clients and therapists. My thoughts on this subject have sprung from over two decades of clinical experience in inpatient psychiatric settings and private practice work and are clearly most applicable to American contexts. However, I believe the principles that have evolved are applicable to art therapists working in the whole range of clinical and community settings.

I begin this discussion by looking at some of the difficulties that may arise at special times of the year. Holiday seasons present art therapists with a number of internal and external problems that can be countertherapeutic. Most prevalent among the countertherapeutic ways of relating with clients for art therapists during the holidays are:

1. **Denial**. Denial is a culturally doomed attempt to ignore the occurrence of a holiday, typified by the art therapist who insists on maintaining a "business as usual" approach, in spite of the mass of social, personal, and cultural pressures upon both the art therapist and her client.

2. **Overcompensation**. Overcompensation is an attempt to produce an ideal holiday experience within the therapy relationship or milieu.

Denying the special-ness of holiday seasons and overcompensating in response to holidays are both approaches based upon false premises. Denial and overcompensation can never be the servants of reality and these approaches often generate inauthentic encounters between art therapists and clients. At best, such inauthentic interactions provide no therapeutic growth. At worst, they promote regressive responses, alternately Pollyanna-sweet and bitterly hostile.

To counteract potentially harmful and obstructive interactions between art therapists and clients, it is imperative to understand the difficulties that holidays can raise for both. Clients and therapists often have a sense that holidays offer an opportunity, or rationalization, for taking a break from treatment. The internal emotional pulls for a therapy-vacation are powerful and magnified because they occur in both therapist and client. Mature art therapists must fight the urge to withdraw from their difficult work with clients. Art therapists certainly need time away from their demanding and often painful therapeutic encounters. However, holiday seasons may not be the best times for extended absences from one's clients. In some circumstances, clients may experience the art therapist's vacation as traumatic abandonment. Abandonment feelings are intensified and multiplied during special times of the year. It is important that art therapists give consideration to the potential effects on the therapeutic relationship of holiday vacations. It is, of course, crucial that art therapists schedule time away from their work, but the timing of vacations can be sensitive to both clients' and art therapist's needs.

Having said that, it is equally important that art therapists not assume responsibility for the real or perceived emotional pain their clients may experience during holiday seasons. Art therapists need to maintain their professional and personal boundaries and allow clients to feel whatever they feel.

Holidays, particularly the Thanksgiving-Christmas-Hanukkah season in America, are stressful for nearly everyone. Cultural images of idealized happy families bombard us and create an expectation of familial harmony that is unreal and can exacerbate tensions. People in therapy are often in strained family circumstances and the strain can be heightened during holiday seasons. Art therapists have to stay focused on the reality of a client's life and not project their own experience of holidays and family onto the client.

At the same time, one can expect that clients' transferences to art therapists may be intensified during the holidays. Few of my clients have reported having had pleasant and positive experiences with these special occasions. On the contrary, it has been typical for their dysfunctional families to become even more dysfunctional during the holidays. A telltale statement from one such client, "It's Christmas, the only day of the whole year that my family can get along," sent warning signals that the holiday would be difficult.

Art therapists must be wary of their own desire to gratify clients, to make them happy, in order to make themselves happy on the holiday. This is a dangerous temptation. Such occasions test the boundaries of client/therapist relationships. If boundaries become blurred, there is always a significant disruption in the therapy process. Appropriate professional boundaries must be maintained in order for the client to remain safe enough in the relationship while trying to cope with the holiday season.

To find a middle ground between denial and overcompensation, the holiday must be recognized, but in a way that is clearly separate from the client's earlier experiences. Staff members of treatment units and art therapists, regardless of their work setting, must establish their own set of traditions that match the realities of client experience of being in therapy during the holidays. Arts therapists often lay the cornerstones for the development of such traditions because of their particular sensitivity to the role of images and rituals within therapeutic relationships. The individual art therapist working in private practice must also make efforts to solidify his or her own sense of celebrative traditions in order to maintain therapeutic boundaries.

The lesser holidays, such as Halloween, Labor Day, and Memorial Day, present fewer problems in therapy. These holidays are generally short in duration and do not expand into an entire season. Therefore they are less disruptive to the therapy process and require less special planning on the part of art therapists. Still, even these lesser holidays demand some measure of forethought. It is again important that the holiday not be ignored, but rather explored for its particular meaning and potential for familial or personal historical significance

For all art therapists, working independently or as part of a treatment team, the Thanksgiving–Christmas–Hanukkah season provides a much more complicated and tumultuous set of difficulties. There is no doubt that this holiday season is fraught with cultural and familial expectations that often serve to intensify and magnify pain, anxiety, and guilt. It is essential that art therapists plan well in advance to explore feelings, expectations, and fears about these holiday seasons with clients before intense feelings arise.

One aspect of the major holiday season is the phenomenon of gift giving. It is important for the art therapist to be clear about his or her policy (or the institutional policy) regarding the giving and receiving of gifts among clients and therapists or clients' families and therapists. Generally, I recommend art therapists avoid the exchange of gifts with clients or families, for such encounters tend to alter the nature of therapeutic relationships. Giving and receiving gifts may shift relationships from a professional to a personal plane. Refusing a gift from a client can be easier to say than to do. Art therapists can save themselves and their clients much discomfort and anxiety by making the boundaries of the relationship clear well in advance of the holiday pressures.

An important factor here is the element of *specialness* in relationship. Art therapists must often contend with their own inner wish to see themselves as unique in the lives of their clients. The wish has a powerful, seductive undertow. Art therapists may see themselves as creative, special individuals and view their work as a significant and special influence in the lives of their clients. It is not surprising that many art therapists are offered gifts. Some in the creative arts therapy professions feel they are underpaid, and generous persons who deserve to be given to. I do not wish to imply this is a conscious belief, but rather an underlying sense. From the viewpoint of the client or the client's family, there may also be an unspoken wish to concretize a special bond with the therapist that is confirmed symbolically by the giving of a gift.

I experienced one example of the complex nature of this dynamic with the parents of an adolescent I'd worked with for over a year in my private practice. The course of therapy had gone well and many of the self-defeating and hostile behaviors of my client had been worked through. I believe the parents genuinely wanted to express their appreciation of my efforts with their daughter. The Christmas gift they chose for me was a bottle of wine. Certainly in our culture this is an often-given gift. However, many of the issues the client and I had explored through her art were related to her father's drinking. The gift of a bottle of wine, therefore, took on potent symbolic overtones. Since the parents chose to give me the wine in the presence of their daughter it made for a complicated therapy drama.

I could see that my client was watching intently for my reaction. I chose to handle this awkward, yet poignant moment by thanking the parents and commenting on the quality of their selection. I added, "but I'm sorry I cannot accept this gift. I really do appreciate your desire to give me something, but I think it's most important that giving and receiving takes place in the therapy between your daughter and me." I did accept the card accompanying the gift and commented that it was a lovely card. The client's father became incensed and left my office without saying another word. The mother was embarrassed and apologized for the father's behavior.

For several sessions after this, my client and I made artwork about the events of that evening. It was significant that this incident sparked her entry into an Al-anon group, which she eventually encouraged her mother to join as well. The bond between the client and her mother eventually led to the father entering Alcoholics Anonymous.

As this vignette illustrates, the simple act of giving, receiving, or refusing a gift has far-reaching meanings. Had I chosen to accept the gift, I would have aligned myself symbolically with the dysfunctional roots of my client's problems. I had no desire to do that. The dynamics of this example are relatively easy to understand. In other instances, the exchange of gifts between clients and therapists may carry subtler but no less significant meaning. It is essential that arts therapists have the potential consequences of accepting or refusing a gift clearly thought through before they happen.

It is imperative that art therapists think deeply about their relationships with clients during holiday seasons. Holidays tend to call up past experiences, childhood memories, and family dynamics that stir potent feelings. Arts therapists need to keep their professional focus clearly on the client and not give in to internal drives or external forces that would sidetrack or disrupt the difficult work at hand. In reality there may be no such thing as a free gift with no strings attached. As difficult as it sounds, the work of therapy takes no vacations.

Chapter XVI

METAVERBAL THERAPY

The Sixteenth Essential–Images are beyond words.

As art therapy students approach their first solo experiences as art therapy group leaders, or individual therapists, one recurrent fear is expressed: *What if I run out of things to say?*

I always have mixed feelings as this fear is spoken. On the one hand, I am amused, for I often marvel at the wealth of therapeutic material contained in clients' images. There is always so much that could be said and never enough time to say it all in one session. On the other hand, the underlying fear suggested by the students' question evokes in me a sense of frustration. I typically put so much effort into stressing the point that the most significant things to happen in any given art therapy session occur between the artist/client, the art process, and the image she creates. From this perspective, nothing at all needs to be said. I tell students over and over again that our words are just the icing on the cake. The main course of the therapeutic meal is served before the art therapist says a word.

The students' question speaks to a central issue in the art therapy profession. How much of what we do can, or should, be put into words? Art therapy has often been described as a *non-verbal* treatment modality.

I have never liked that description because it defines the field through the negative. Saying that art therapy is a non-verbal modality indicates what art therapy is not, rather than what it is. I much prefer to describe art therapy as a *metaverbal* treatment modality. Metaverbal means *beyond words.*

When art therapy students want me to explain the distinction between *non-verbal* and *metaverbal,* I ask them to recall a significant event in their lives. Some remember a birthday, others a wedding, and others the death of a member of their family. In each case, I ask them to describe the scene and to tell what happened. Students share memories of people, activities, places, and so on. I then ask them to recount verbatim a specific conversation that occurred at the time of the event. Invariably this is difficult, if not impossible, to do. Where their descriptions of people, actions, and places were rich and full of life and color, their verbal recitations are sparse and difficult to recount.

The point of this exercise is to demonstrate that most people retain image memories longer than they retain words. I am convinced that life's deeper moments and more meaningful experiences are nearly impossible to put into words.

An example of the difficulty of putting meaningful experience into words for me was the births of my children. After the events, I tried to tell anyone and everyone who would listen all about these miraculous happenings and my feelings about them. As hard as I tried to convey the depth, the awe, the mystery, my words were inadequate. Now, looking back, I cannot recall anything at all being said in the birthing room, but I have vibrant images of holding my son and daughter for the first time. These experiences were beyond the capacity of words to describe.

In our culture, we are bombarded by words. We see them on signs, in the newspaper, in books and magazines, on the computer screen. We hear them on the radio, on television, and in conversation. There are so many words in just one day. It is impossible to retain them all. The sheer volume of words we receive has rendered them impotent.

We can only imagine what it must have been like when a primitive man or woman first uttered a sound meaning *water* and was understood by another. What power, to speak the name of water and call up the image of water in the mind of another! The word was a symbol, the embodiment of the thing it represented (Samuels & Samuels, 1975, p. 17).

Word is derived from the Greek root *logos,* referring to the controlling principle of the universe as manifested in speech. In Christian theology, *the Word* is the eternal thought of God.

When examined from these historic perspectives, words appear to have had rather a different weight than is currently given them in our culture. Perhaps this has to do with words' early connection with image. The image-words of fire, water, beast or food had much to do with the ultimate concerns of primitive people, i.e., their survival. Today words are often used to disguise, euphemize, and obscure real meanings.

The real substance of our work as art therapists takes place among the client/artist, the media, the process of creating, and the art therapist. In a radical sense, I believe it would be possible for art therapists to do significant work without speaking at all.

In hospitals, clinics, and treatment programs, there are many professionals whose primary way of relating to the client is through verbal interaction. Art therapists' special gift to the treatment of clients is the provision of a metaverbal arena in which to form relationships.

I encourage my students to be skeptical of their desire to talk with clients. The wish to say the *right thing* or the fear of saying the *wrong thing* may represent a distrust of the power of artistic processes.

When students worry they will run out of things to say in an art therapy session, I encourage them to trust the artwork. By this, I mean to continually refer to the art piece, to look for ways to relate to the artist and the piece without words. Art therapists can respond to artworks through movement, sound, poetry, and music or by making art in reaction to clients' work. This may be difficult because educational systems rely so heavily on written and spoken words. When art therapy educators attempt to teach an approach that does not depend upon skillful manipulation of words, they must wrestle with finding new methods of instruction. We cannot simply talk about not talking so much. This is why art making, dancing, moving, and making sounds can be so important to art therapy educational processes.

I have challenged the need that many art therapists have to talk with clients about images (Moon, 1995, 1997). I firmly believe we could do most of our work with clients without speaking at all. However, it is a reality that professional human service disciplines depend heavily on words to describe therapeutic processes. Most practicing art therapists and art therapy students function in treatment settings predominantly populated by colleagues from verbal disciplines. Still, it is critical for art therapists to think about images and about language. For those students who will soon be out in the world treating clients, this is an important subject. All of the good work done with clients may come to nothing if the art therapist cannot put into words what occurs in the therapeutic encounter. Insurance companies may not be willing to pay for art therapy services and employers may not take the profession seriously if art therapists cannot articulate the nature of the work.

This is tricky business, for I believe the best of what happens between therapists, clients, and their images is beyond verbal description. It's a lot like trying to find words to describe making love, or being hugged by one's children. There are few words to describe such events.

Poems, dramas, dances, sculptures, paintings, and drawings are not intellectual constructs. They are glimpses of the inner life of the human beings who created them. Each pencil line, every dissonance, and every spot of color are announcements to the self and to the rest of humanity that *I am*. The artist, regardless of media, proclaims to the world, *I have something to say*.

The essence of an artwork is often indescribable in words. Just what did Hopper mean to say in *Nighthawks?* What exactly was e.e. cummings trying to tell us in *Anyone Lived in a Pretty How Town?* These questions can inspire lengthy discussion, but I am wary of anyone who claims to know the answer. The configuration of the artist as a biological, social, cultural, familial, physical, psychological, internally dynamic creator is overwhelmingly complex. Perhaps the most an audience or beholder can do is catch a wisp of the multifaceted communication of the artist. From such glimpses come the first fumbling words of a dialogue between the artist and the beholder.

As art therapists viewing works made by clients, we must struggle to find words that focus the expressed thought, the feelings, the physical effort of the artist, and the soul of the artistic product. I encourage my students to approach every piece of art with a sense of reverence for the story that has been told, as mysterious as it may be. Each time a client scrawls images on the page with chalk, each time she struggles with pen in hand to find the next line of her poem, each time he dabs a brush and smears color across the canvas, there is proclaimed to the world: *I know something, I have something to say*. Inwardly the artist may wonder, will anyone listen, will anyone understand? As art therapists approach such proclamations, we must respect their power and earnestly seek to understand their metaverbal messages.

Originally words were powerful enough to instigate action or call up images essential for survival. For evidence of this power, one needs only to witness the first word of many infants, *Mama*. The child speaks the name of that which is essential for his or her own safety and nurturance. What a powerful word this is! Unfortunately, words have also come to be a means of creating distance between people. Words can be used as a way to remove oneself from the experience of life.

Originally the practice of psychotherapy was described as the "talking cure." However, art psychotherapists have become ever more concerned with the use of words that limit and constrict experience rather than those that broaden expression.

The Missouri slogan, "Show Me," embodies our skepticism of words. We long for observable facts, measurable data, and quantifiable results. Our language and thinking, heavily influenced by the scientific method, have become linear and fact-oriented. In the therapy professions, there is a tendency to use words in an effort to describe, contain, and make understandable. As we try to describe our clients' dysfunctions and explain behaviors, we often leave no room for the imagination, the ambiguous, and paradoxical. Metaphorical glimpses and wisps of insight have become antithetical to the scientific method (Moon, C., 1988). It is as if some believe that if they can explain, if they are knowledgeable enough and if their language can accurately describe phenomena, they will be in control.

I have described the phenomenon of imagicide as the tendency to confine, define, and constrict the images of our clients (Moon, 1995). To do so is to kill the power of the image. Whenever an art therapist tries to explain and label a client's image, she deludes herself into believing that by describing the image, she will somehow know the client in a deeper way. In fact, such explanations take the art therapist further away from the client's experience. The more an art therapist tries intellectually to grasp the meaning of the client's image, the further she removes herself from the multiple potentialities of the image.

It is my sense that in the western world, we have been taught to seek information that can be proven through reason and observation. We have been instructed to be wary of mysteries, paradoxes, and ambiguous forces. We tend to compartmentalize things, to put things into categories: right, wrong, good and bad, thoughts and feelings. I believe our culture has a difficult time appreciating the possibilities of things being both good and bad.

As an art therapist, I believe the images of my clients, no matter how painful, horrific, or frightening, are healthy expressions. Art making does not create an image within a client. On the contrary, art making frees the image. Art making brings the dark, painful, and monstrous to light. Making art is a form of survival, a celebration of life. Clients reach deep within themselves and bring out their pain, their struggle, and their courage. Therefore art therapists must not regard images as signs of pathology, but rather as symbols of self-transformation. Clients' images need to be there, to be seen, and art therapists have to privilege to be with them.

The language I use in the presence of my clients and their artworks is not definitive. It is the language of metaphor. My words serve to attach me to the client and the image. My conversation validates publicly: I am here, I have seen, and I will stay with you.

Over the past 27 years, I have developed some measure of proficiency in using the clinical language of the psychiatric milieu. I can speak with confidence of diagnostic categories from the DSM. I can converse about symptoms and observable behaviors. I know how to write clinical observations acceptable to third-party payers and I can talk with colleagues about a variety of psychotherapeutic theories and treatment approaches. Clinical language is the meeting ground for the helping professions, but it is incomplete. The lively language of the arts complements it.

A Digression

Sarah was only 15 when I first met her. She was a pretty girl with thick, curly brown hair. My first impression of her was of a bright, cheerful, and pleasant young woman, but there was something else in her eyes. She had a sullen, smoldering look that contradicted everything else about her.

When she came to the studio she was immediately excited about the prospect of painting. "I've never done that before, but I've always wanted to," she said.

"Good," I replied. "Let's get to work on building a canvas." I almost never used pre-stretched canvases or canvas boards in the studio. I taught people to use the miter-box saw to cut 2 x 2s at 45degree angles. I helped clients nail and brace the stretcher frame and then shared with them the struggles of white knuckle canvas stretching.

Sarah was good at these things. Although she was a small girl, she insisted on cutting the wood without my assistance and once she understood the mechanics of stretching canvas she took over.

When her canvas was built, she gessoed the surface and then asked, "What's next?"

"For the rest of this session, why don't you think about what you want to paint? You might make some sketches."

"But I already know what I'm going to paint," she said.

I replied, "Well, could you sketch it out for me so I'll know how I can be helpful?"

"No. I don't want your help and I don't want you to know what I am going to paint."

The next day she came into the studio, placed her blank canvas on an easel, gathered paints and brushes, and began to work.

"What are you going to paint?" I asked.

She looked at me with mild irritation. "Do you know anything about Nietzsche?"

I was a bit surprised, having never been asked the question by an adolescent client before. "Yes," I said. "I know a little bit about him."

She stepped back from the canvas. "I'm going to paint the death of God."

"Hmmm. That's a big subject," I said.

"Not for me," she replied. That was the end of our conversation on that day.

The image that took form was of a triangle with its point near the bottom of the canvas. It was outlined in dark gray. Sarah dipped her hands in green and red paint and pressed them around the outside of the triangle. She overlapped these colors, which resulted in a chaotic layering of handprints.

At the bottom of the triangle, Sarah painted a dark blue night sky with tiny white stars. A small burnt sienna figure huddled at the very tip of the triangle's point.

The last thing she did to this painting was to again immerse her right hand in deep red paint and then to make one large arching red smear across the top of the canvas.

As I watched her I was reminded of the scene from the movie *The Ten Commandments* as the members of Moses' family gathered in their house. One person was sent out to smear lamb's blood across the doorframe in order to insure the family would be passed over. It was quite an image.

Sarah sat before her painting. Blood-like paint trickled from her hands, across her wrists and onto her forearm. She cried. Her body shook.

* * *

How do art therapists explain events such as those described above to other members of the treatment team? It is essential for art therapists to hold in tension the polarities of language. In order to function in the world of helping professions, we must find words that enable others to glimpse the *metaverbal* nature of our work. Yet, we must do so in the knowledge that no words will ever adequately describe or contain a work of art.

When I went to the psychiatric team meeting on the day Sarah painted *The Death of God*, I became uneasy. The general consensus of the team members was that Sarah was not really engaged in treatment. Inside my head the image of *The death of God* flashed on and off like a neon sign. What would I say if the doctor asked me what Sarah's painting meant? I did not know what it meant. I just knew it had meaning. What would I say if the psychologist asked, "Is this indicative of psychopathology?" Would I look foolish to my colleagues if I told them how she placed her hands in the paint and on the canvas, and how her body shook as the tears fell on her blouse?

Something happened there . . . something happened.

The purpose of words is to evoke images. In the clinical setting, I sometimes think of myself as an archaeologist of language. I carefully dig through the verbal debris, searching for the long-lost image. I look to poetry, fables, and metaphors. I look for words that are alive with expressive power. I learn from the language of religions and from the rock-and-roll lyricists of today. I struggle to find words that allow images to speak through me. I make no attempt to speak for the image.

Chapter XVII

THE MIRROR

The Seventeenth Essential–Art therapy students are both the object of, and subject of, inquiry.

I have used the image of "the canvas mirror" as a metaphor of the introspective processes that are the foundation of art making and art therapy education (Moon, 1995). "There have been periods of my life when I have looked into the mirror and found images of courage and integrity. I have also seen open wounds, loneliness, and cowardice . . . When I try to run from the canvas reflection I am intensely aware that I am running . . . there is no escape" (p. 179).

The image of the mirror (Fig. 29) has emerged again for me in writing this book. It is intended as an affirmation that self-reflection and self-transparency are cornerstones of our work as art therapists and as art therapy educators.

As I prepare to lecture at various colleges and universities throughout the country, I always ask faculty members to describe the nature of their relationships with students. I want to know if my approach to education will be consistent with what the students have already experienced. Author and art therapist Shaun McNiff has described the experience of reading my writings as having been invited into a confessional cell. Prior to his comment, it had never occurred to me that what I wrote would be read as that intimate. Reflecting upon his feedback, it is clear to me that this intimate perspective may describe my position as an art therapy educator as well. I make no attempt to write or teach from a detached or purely intellectual stance. I do not believe therapy of any sort can be taught or learned that way.

In art therapy education, intellectual objectivity is important, but there must be more. The art therapy student is both *studier* and *studied*, both the object and subject of inquiry. The same is true for the art therapy educator. The educator does not merely cite appropriate references, but also must be willing to be the focus of critical research and

130

interrogation from the student. This is not easy work.

George Gibbs, who for many years was the chaplain at Harding Hospital in Worthington, Ohio, criticizes the tendency of authors of "therapy books" to present only their success stories. Gibbs suggests that as promoters of a point of view or philosophy, authors seldom mention the client they failed to help, the clients who resisted the writer's best efforts at benevolent assistance. George's point is well taken, and I would include myself as one of the "success storytellers." I do it again in this book, for I am arguing in favor of particular points of view regarding art therapy education and practice.

Still, I must be honest. Over the years, I've been directly involved in the treatment of nearly a dozen human beings who, despite my best efforts and the efforts of many others, committed suicide. These remembered names and faces are dramatic testament that there are failures in this work. Sometimes the psychotherapy, art therapy, psychopharmacology, intensive nursing care, sophisticated psychological testing, adjunctive therapies, and family therapy all added together are not enough.

The suicide of a client is graphic evidence of failure, but there are many more subtle failures that we art therapists must endure. We are not gods. Ultimately, it is the client who does the hardest work in therapy. It really is the client's success when the therapy works and his or her failure when it does not. Still, we therapists cannot divorce ourselves from pride in effective work and disappointment in unsatisfactory progress.

Perhaps most of the case study literature in our field details therapeutic success. This is understandable. No one relishes having students or peers read about their failures. Yet this is unfortunate, for the reality is that many people who seek art therapy do not improve as a result of their therapy. Some people get worse and some people make no change at all. Fortunately, many get better.

The focus of this chapter is on looking in the mirror. Part of the process of self-examination entails exploring one's shortcomings. It was not an easy chapter to include, but it is an essential aspect of the arts therapy professions. It is important that students know there will be times in their professional lives when they will feel bad about their work. They will be frustrated by their own impotence. They will be wounded from time to time by their inability to *make* someone change.

I include here a vignette of failure. It represents a composite picture

Figure 29. I have seen images of courage and cowardice.

of a host of failures. They are my failures, my colleagues' failures, and my clients' failures.

What to Do About Jane

Jane was 24 when I first met her. She'd been referred to my private practice by a psychiatrist from a large general hospital. She was quite depressed and had been unresponsive to the psychiatrist's interventions. Her father had died about six months prior and she had recently been in a car accident.

During her first session, she completed a large chalk drawing she titled, *My Inner and Outer Worlds.* She had covered the page in black and then smeared blue across the black background. The emotional tone of the drawing was depressing and bleak. In a variety of ways, I tried to explore with Jane the meaning of this black and blue image. I worked very hard in that first session. In retrospect, I see now that Jane hardly worked at all. It was as if she presented this dark image and then disowned it.

At the close of the session I encouraged her to keep her drawing, to take it with her.

Bruce: Maybe you should save this. It may be the first symbolic step of our journey together.

Jane: I don't want it. You'd better keep it for us.

Bruce: Are you sure? I know it represents hard feelings, but someday you may wish you'd kept it.

Jane: No, I don't have any place in my apartment to store it. You can keep it or throw it away.

In this small interchange, Jane had subtly set the parameters of our relationship. In a sense, she had written the contract that I was to fulfill. It would be my job to take care of, to hold, to store, and dispose of her bad feelings. She did not have room for them.

Unfortunately, I did not understand these messages until many months had passed. During that time, Jane created a host of images related to her negative self-view, the tragedies of her life, and the mistreatment she received at the hands of others. She drew or painted these pictures and then dumped them on my floor, soliciting my prescription.

An example: She drew a picture of herself and her roommate engaged in a heated argument about getting up in the morning. Jane had somehow gotten her roommate to be responsible for awakening her in time for work. Jane said that her roommate was always harsh in the morning and that she (Jane) resented being awakened so rudely. The picture was filled with two angry mouths casting fire towards each other.

I suggested she might buy an alarm clock and waken herself. Jane obediently did so, but came in the following week furious because her roommate had not reminded her to set the alarm clock. As a result, Jane had been late for work on two occasions. Her boss was angry with her and she was angry at her roommate and at me.

In the course of her therapy, Jane presented situation after situation like this. I began to set aside time in my schedule before her appointments so that I could prepare for Jane's visits. I began to dread her appointments.

After some time, it occurred to me that I was working a whole lot harder on Jane's therapy than she was. Once this became clear to me, I was able to develop what I considered to be a more coherent strategy for dealing with her. My plan was to do less.

As Jane entered my studio she said, "It's been a horrible week. I've felt so bad, I haven't been able to go to work. I haven't worked on my journal, haven't painted. I haven't been able to do anything."

"Sounds bad," I said.

"So what do you want me to do today, Bruce?"

"I don't know, Jane."

"What do you mean, you don't know?"

"I don't know what you should do, Jane."

Silence

Jane angrily asked, "What is this? You're supposed to help me, not just sit there. You're acting like my old counselor.

"How am I like him?"

"You're not doing anything to help me." Jane replied.

"What do you want me to do, Jane?"

"I don't know. Tell me to draw something or ask about my journal. Something!"

"Jane, I am doing, and have been doing something for a long time now. I've been here with you. I've never missed an appointment. For that matter, you've really accomplished a lot, too."

"Like what?"

"You've maintained our relationship for a year and a half. It hasn't been easy, but you've stuck with it.

"But I still feel like crap." She exclaimed.

The rest of the session continued in much this same way. Jane telephoned to cancel the next session. She rescheduled but failed to keep the next appointment. About six weeks went by before she called again. She wanted to tell me she'd decided that she needed a new therapist and she'd found a "wonderful woman psychiatrist" whose office was in her neighborhood.

I suggested we might meet at least once more in order to bring our work together to a close. Jane coolly declined, saying that she saw no reason for such a meeting.

I learned later that Jane went to only a couple of sessions with the new therapist and then decided that she needed more help than the psychiatrist was willing to provide. So it goes.

This was a disturbing failure for me as an art therapist. Not only was I unable to help Jane make the changes she wanted to make, but the relationship I had thoughtfully nurtured ended in such an abrupt and unclean manner that it raised questions about the authenticity of the relationship all along. Did we ever really have a relationship? How could she terminate the therapy in such a way? Was I completely fooled? What could I have done differently? How . . . what . . . why . . . should? These questions plague me as they plague all caregivers. Was it my failure, or Jane's failure, or our failure, or no one's failure? Or, was this experience just a blip in Jane's long history of therapy? I do not know, and for now I must be content with my inability to know.

As an educator, I see it as my responsibility to guide my students toward a realistic view of the art therapy profession. It is essential to help them develop a truthful view of the work. A realistic view includes the joy of success and the fact of failure.

In the medical community, doctors must contend with their own finite capabilities. The ultimate reminder of this is the death of a patient. It is one of the tragedies of medicine that technology has fostered a system of denial about the limitations of the physician. Even with the most sophisticated life support systems available, eventually, ultimately, inevitably the patient dies.

We arts therapists have no such life-support technology. Still the analogy is apt. Ultimately, the work of getting better is the client's work to do. Many clients will improve and many will not. This represents a paradoxical situation for the art therapist. What we do is incredibly important, but all we do is sometimes not enough.

A former colleague, Dr. Henry Leuchter, used to tell me, "Bruce, out of every ten people you meet, two are going to like you no matter what you do. Two are not going to like you no matter what you do. The rest are up for grabs." Perhaps this is the way it is with clients as well. Two might get better no matter what you do. Two might get worse. The rest are up for grabs.

Chapter XVIII

THE ROLE OF METAPHOR

The Eighteenth Essential–Art therapists are *metaphoreticians.*

Art therapist look at, listen to, and share stories through metaphoric action. By making art, we work with, play with, and enact the salient themes of the therapeutic journey with our clients. It is our critical responsibility to see and respond to the metaphoric messages that emerge through the sharing of artistic images. We barely need to talk at all.

Essential to the healing capacity of the art therapist is the use of metaphor. The metaphors of art therapists are not solely of the spoken variety. In art therapy, metaphors can be found in both actions and objects in which one thing (the client) is described in the terms of another (the image or artistic process). The visual metaphors of art therapy hold in tension the potential for multiple interpretations, their purpose being to illuminate truths about clients' feelings, thoughts, and experiences.

By our very nature we art therapists are *metaphoreticians.* Our work is to interact with the graphic symbolic images and actions of our clients. By doing so we respond to the metaphors of our clients within the therapy milieu.

* * *

A young man was referred to an art therapy group. In the referral note the psychiatrist explained that James had been in individual psychotherapy for three months and in a long-term treatment unit for adolescents for more than four months but had made little progress because of his very rigid defenses. Discussing the situation further with the psychiatrist, I learned that James typically avoided his psychotherapy sessions. When he did attend, he often walked out after 10 minutes or so. The psychiatrist was frustrated by this 16-year-old's defiant attitude, best summed up in the client's words, "Fuck therapy. I want to go home."

The therapist had employed many approaches in an attempt to engage James. At first he had assumed a non-directive manner. When he made no headway with this approach, he had become more actively supportive and friendly. In turn, James was provided with many opportunities to reject the therapist and devalue the process. The therapist then had shifted to a more directive and confrontive mode, but this too had served only to increase the client's resistance to self-exploration and sharing. In short, the client was stuck in a resistive stance. His insurance resources were being drained and the treatment team members were afraid time was running out for James.

James' history included truancy, vandalism, drug and alcohol abuse, and violent behavior with peers and family members. The psychiatrist feared that James would end up in jail or dead if James did not make some changes in his life. Hospitalization was regarded as a "last chance" effort to turn things around.

As my co-therapist and I discussed James' entry into our group, we made careful note of the failed therapeutic interventions. We decided that we would (1) avoid confrontation whenever possible, and (2) try to engage James through the metaphors of his images, whatever they might be.

In the first art group session that James attended, we began by asking the group members to cover their large (3' x 3') papers with red and brown chalk. They were then asked to smear the colors together, making a solid red-brown surface. James was skeptical and made several quiet, devaluing comments to his peers. However, since everyone else in the group was working at the task, James complied. My co-therapist and I made mental note of his comments but did not intervene or respond to his negativity.

Then I said, "Now what we have here is a segment of a brick wall. Your task is to apply whatever graffiti or slogans or drawings you'd want to put on your brick wall." James seemed to like this idea. It was representative of vandalizing, which he knew how to do. He quickly picked up a white chalk and scrawled, "Fuck therapy." He then drew the anarchy symbol, a smoldering marijuana cigarette, a bottle of beer, and a red smear. He told the boy next to him that the smear was a bloodstain from where someone had hit the wall with his fist.

As the group members talked about their images, my co-therapist and I made every attempt to honor the drawings and their content. When James shared his drawing, I commented (staying with the metaphor), "James, it appears your wall has had some very rough experiences."

James replied, "Wha' ya mean?"

"It looks like someone has hit this wall, and I see that the wall has been around drugs and alcohol."

James groaned, "Like I always say, fuck this." He quickly looked to his peers for support of his challenging attitude.

I went on, "James, you know in this group we always take things that are drawn very seriously."

He sighed, "Don't go bein' therapeutic with me. I just drew this shit. It don't mean anything."

"It's okay if that's what you think. But I have this idea that what we draw is kind of a portrait of who we are."

(James stared.)

I said, "Of course, I don't know what to make of this Fuck Therapy stuff. You do realize this is a biological impossibility?"

The members of the group chuckled. James scowled, "What in hell are you talking about?"

"You do realize that it is not possible to have sexual intercourse with therapy."

At this, James and the other boys in the group began to laugh. My co-therapist and I laughed too. Then I shifted my attention back to James' image. "But really, James, I see the blood on your wall and I know somebody hit you, I mean your wall, pretty hard."

James replied, "Yeah, lots of times. So what?

"It looks like this is a strong wall, James. I'm glad you have it. It seems like you have needed your wall to protect you."

"Yeah, I guess."

That was the beginning of James' journey into himself. Over the next few months, he led us over a path past scenes of abuse from an alcoholic father, metaphorically depicted as a monster who "steps on baby chicks." Episodes of destructive sexual acting out were represented in the symbolic forms of animals forced to share a cavern/prison.

As James grew more comfortable in the group and his story became more apparent through his images, he gradually dropped his hostile,

Figure 30. The clarity of communication presented in the object.

resistant behavior. He began to take his drawings to his individual therapist, where he told his tale again. As his old distancing maneuvers were abandoned, he allowed himself to become attached to the nursing staff, activity therapists, and others on the treatment team.

* * *

The classic definition of a metaphor is that it is a figure of speech containing an implied comparison, in which a word or a phrase ordinarily and primarily used for one thing is applied to another. In our work as creative arts therapists and educators, this definition is insufficient, for it ties one to verbal constructs. James' metaphors were not made of language. They were forged of images made of chalk and paper. Without them, I do not believe he would ever have been able to benefit from his hospital stay or make use of therapy.

Metaphors are images. This concept is a key element, a most potent element of the art therapy discipline. Images are metaphors containing an inherent comparison in which one thing is used to describe another. James' metaphors, without which no therapy would have occurred, were his images of monsters and chicks, prisons and caves, walls and graffiti.

As arts therapists, educators, and students, we are obliged to develop a reverence for image metaphors. We need not attempt to imprison metaphor through vocabulary. Instead, we can foster a sense of awe and commit ourselves to the notion that the image can, and should, *just be.* I do not propose an anti-verbal doctrine; rather, I am calling for a strong pro-metaverbal faith in image metaphors. If paint flows in the veins of art therapists, metaphors are in their hearts.

All things we create are partial self-portraits. Any image that comes through us is both an independent entity and a description of its creator. The arts therapist needs only to look and be with the images of the client. McNiff suggests that the purpose of the metaphor is to elucidate or make clear. The need to talk, or translate images into words, is a phenomenon that often makes me uneasy with colleagues in art therapy and other disciplines as well. It seems to indicate that the therapist does not trust the image. When art therapists value the clarity of communication presented in the object or process of art making, we hardly need to talk at all.

Chapter XIX

THE ROLE OF LOVE

The Nineteenth Essential–Love is the will to attend.

Don't talk of love, I've heard the word before . . .
Paul Simon

For the most part, this book is about educating would-be art therapists in the discipline of the profession. This chapter will explore what lies behind, or perhaps beneath, the discipline. We must ask ourselves, what is the *driving force*, the *push*, and the *enthusiasm* for our work? I believe that driving force is *love*. I feel a little uneasy saying so. I have looked at many degree-program catalogues and public relations materials from universities and have failed to find any direct mention or even veiled reference to love. Still, I believe it is the force that pushes art therapy educators, pulls art therapists, and seduces students of the profession. Of course, I am aware that by attempting to explore love, I will be discussing the immeasurable, illogical, and mysterious. According to Peck (1978) in addressing the subject of love, ". . . we will be attempting to examine the unexamineable and to know the unknowable" (p. 81). Even so, I think it is essential that an attempt be made to grapple with this driving force, for it is surely the foundation upon which many, if not all therapeutic endeavors are built. Therapists receive money for what they do, but it is clear that most of us are not in the profession to get rich. There are other, more direct routes to that end, ones with fewer headaches and heartaches at that.

Countless artists have created works of art, paintings, poems, songs, dances, and dramas in an attempt to express and/or define love. These artistic expressions seem, however, only to reveal various facets of love. Love may be too big a subject to be understood and too deep to be confined by language. In *The Road Less Traveled*, Peck (1978) offers the following definition of love: "The will to extend one's self for the purpose of nurturing one's own or another's spiritual growth" (p. 81).

I offer yet another definition of love, with proper acknowledgement that it is an inadequate and clumsy attempt. I define love as *the will to attend, to be with, one's self and the self of others.*

I have had many professional contacts with members of other action-oriented therapies such as occupational therapy, recreation therapy, horticulture therapy, and work therapy. From these encounters, I have developed a deep commitment to the maxim, "Actions speak louder than words." Therefore I begin my definition of love with "the will to. . . ." By using the word "will," there is an implicit integration of intent or wish and action. *Will* is a wish so powerful that it must become an act. *Will* is a precursor to action. One cannot simply want to love. Love must be manifested in action towards others and the self. Will also connotes free choice. To attend to another, to love, is an act of choice. I do not have to do it, and in fact, there are probably many times that I choose, for one reason or another, not to attend. Paradoxically there are moments, particularly in the art therapy studio, when I am deeply attuned to a client without my conscious effort. At some deep level, I have chosen to openly be with the client. Thereby I have chosen to love.

Implicit in my definition of love is a quality of give-and-take, a dialogue. It is impossible to be genuinely attentive to another if you are not attentive to yourself. In the context of the art therapy studio, "being with" the images created by the client enhances the ability to be with one's own images. This creates an artistic, circular process of loving awareness.

Let me offer an additional comment regarding my definition of love as the will to attend to one's self and the self of another. Although love is an act of will, a choice, the force itself is without a goal or purpose. One loves for the sake of loving; one attends to self or other for the sake of attending. Loving does not bring material gain or power or prestige. It brings only itself, and that is the mystery.

The clients who come to art therapy often have been victimized by people who should have loved them. Clients come bearing emotional scars, the remnants of physical, sexual, or emotional abuse. They come hungry for attention and yet are frightened, guarded, and defended from love's curative effects. This is why educational programs designed to teach the creative arts therapies must begin to wrestle with the driving force of love. It is not enough to teach mastery of media, developmental theory, psychotherapeutic technique, documentation procedures, and the history of the profession. We must begin a dialogue with students as early as possible about the deepest and most noble motivation of the discipline, love.

The creation of art is itself an act of love. As the artist dips the brush into the pigment and moves color to the empty canvas, an image begins its incredible pilgrimage from deep within to without. Lines, shapes and colors are added; the image takes form and is born. There is a continuous push and pull among the artist, the medium, and the canvas. The image emerges from imagination, conflict, and emotion. The process, this attending to, is deeply moving, so filled with subtle nuance that it cannot be accurately described. The artist alone experiences the full meaning of the unfolding event. It is the task of the art therapist to be with the client/artist, acting as midwife to the birth of self. The art therapist must love in such moments. Doing so provides a healing, restorative milieu for the client.

Ideally, the art therapy context is a community of love. It may be a community of three—client, therapist, and artwork—or a larger community in the case of expressive therapy groups. Existential meanings can be found only through transcending the self in community. Creative acts can best be appreciated and stimulated in the realm of relationships.

The artist client establishes the parameters of her love through the performance of creative endeavors. Ideally, she acts out of love as she creates; love of self and love for the community. The art therapist, through acceptance, praise, or confrontation, acts out her love by seriously engaging with the art and its creator.

The mystery of this creative interaction among artist, image, and therapist is that such love is neither earned nor imposed. Creation and attention are acts of grace, not forced or deserved. The mystery is felt as the client steps away from the canvas in order to get a different perspective. It is sensed in the fleeting moments as the artist signs the work, knowing that the signature does not denote "I did this," but "I am this." The mystery is present as others pause to look, to see, and be with the image.

Being attended to sharpens one's ability to value self and others. Both the loved and the lover see the world with new eyes. All images and actions are enhanced and given meaning through the grace of love. From meaning comes the motivation to create again. From creation comes meaning, comes motivation, comes creation . . . on and on the loving goes.

A Digression

Diana had been in the expressive arts therapy group only twice before. The group consisted of seven adolescents from the dual-diagnosis unit at the hospital, and myself. Clients admitted to the unit suffered from psychiatric disorders severe enough to warrant inpatient hospitalization and significant drug or alcohol abuse symptoms. This was often a difficult group, resistive and devaluing toward treatment. Complicating matters further, Diana and two of her peers had been ordered into the hospital by the juvenile court system. The general emotional tone of the group was hostile.

On this particular day, I'd chosen to introduce the drawing exercise, "The Emotional Mirror" as the focus of the session. One boy, Dave, perhaps the most negative and hostile member of the group, drew a large "F." "U." Beside the letters he added a stick figure with a brown ambiguous shape (perhaps representing a pile of horse manure) where the head should be. The stick figure held a piece of chalk in one hand. I quickly grasped the overt message to me: "Fuck you, shithead."

Diana and her peers in the group also got the point of Dave's drawing and were snickering and whispering among themselves, no doubt wondering what my reaction would be. Internally, I felt a flash of anger. A voice within me shouted, *How dare you do that in here?* Another interior voice prodded me to confront Dave with the harshest reprimand I could muster. But a third voice whispered, *What you do in the next few minutes will have real impact on the life of this group. Respond as lovingly as you can, Bruce. Don't react!*

I finished my drawing and sat down, silently surveying the works around me. From each of the seven emotional mirrors, fierce and painful images glared back at me. Diana's drawing was a representation of a backseat car window with the bottoms of two feet hanging out. The scene was surrounded by harsh black and purple slashing lines. There was a red line, perhaps a trickle of blood, seeping through the crack between the door and the frame of the car.

Since so much attention was being focused on Dave's drawing, I decided to begin the group dialogue with his image.

I said, "Well, Dave, your drawing seems to have stirred the interest of the group."

"Yeah, so what!"

"It's quite a strong image. Dave, would you like to say anything about it?

He responded, "Don't play yer damn games with me, man. I ain't in the mood.

"I'm not playing games, Dave, I mean it. That is a very strong image. The whole point of being in this group is to express your self. You certainly did."

Clearly this was not the reaction Dave, or anyone else in the group, had expected to get from me.

Dave said, "So wha' you gonna do about it?"

"I'm not going to do anything, Dave. I'm just being with it."

He grimaced, "Huh?"

"Dave, you know I believe that everything we create is sort of a self-portrait. When I look at your 'Fuck You Shit Head' I really get a sense of how you feel about things. It must be really hard.

"What!?" he exclaimed.

I went on, "Really, thanks for sharing with the group. It's a gift, to let people know how you feel about yourself and the world."

Then, without hesitation, giving Dave no time to respond, I asked who would like to share their drawing next. Diana said, quietly, "I'll go."

She stared at her image for a few moments. "I don't know why I drew this. At first, when I saw what Dave was doing, I thought this would be funny."

(long pause)

I said, "And now . . ."

"Now I don't know."

"It doesn't look very funny to me, Diana."

One of the other girls laughed nervously and said, "Looks like Friday night at the Drive-in to me."

I said, "It doesn't look like very much fun, though. Look at all those lines around the outside. They look violent. And that looks like it might be blood coming out of the door. No, it doesn't look funny, Diana." I looked from the drawing to Diana. Tears were running down her face, making wet spatters on her blouse. The room was quiet and still.

She said, "I was raped when I was 13." A sob escaped her as she continued, "Since then I've put my feet up for just about any guy who asked."

From across the room, Dave said, "That really sucks. You're too good for that, Diana. Nobody should treat you that way!"

Diana turned toward him, "It's not them anymore. Didn't you hear what Bruce said about your drawing, Dave? It's me! It's how I treat me. Her sobbing continued.

One of the other group members fidgeted in her seat, "Can we go on now?"

"In a minute," I said. "But right now it's important that we let Diana have her time. I know it's hard, but she needs to feel what she feels, and I need to be here with her."

Dave said, "Yeah, me too!"

And so the group sat with Diana as she cried.

As Diana was preparing for her discharge from the hospital, she reminded me of that session. She told me her drawing was important for her, but what had really made the difference that day was that I had not gotten into a "scene" with Dave. She said, "I decided that if you could be nice to him with what he drew, it would be okay for me to talk about that stuff."

As art therapists we work with images that come from the innermost parts of ourselves, and our clients. I do not believe it is an overstatement to describe this work as an act of love. In fact, it may be an understatement to define it as anything less than love. Making art and doing therapy both require great effort. Both activities call for self-transcendence and challenge basic human inertia. Facing this challenge for the sake of the client and for one's self is an act of love and courage.

As I stand before the chalk-smeared paper and see what my client has done, I attend to her story. I am awed by her work, her courage, and the love that encircles client, therapist, artist, and image.

Love is the will to attend and it is the driving force of art therapy. This is an essential concept that must be conveyed within the halls of higher education.

Chapter XX

THE ROLE OF ASSESSMENT

**The Twentieth Essential–In art therapy,
assessment is a process, not an event.**

Art therapists working in institutional settings are frequently asked to administer art therapy assessments for the purposes of initial evaluation of a client or helping to clarify diagnostic impressions. Art therapists in private practice often utilize art assessment procedures in the initial stages of therapy in order to help in the design of treatment plans and to clarify clinical impressions of a client.

Art therapy assessments can offer a unique view of the client. It is important for art therapy educational settings to prepare students to be sensitive observers of artistic behavior and to help them learn to present their observations professionally, creatively, and compassionately. It is essential that students be provided with ample practical experience in observation and articulation.

In the summer of 1988, I became a member of a long-range planning task force with a two-fold charge: (1) to make recommendations regarding the design a physical environment for the short-term hospitalization of children and adolescents ages four to 17 years; (2) to outline the evaluative and treatment services for the short-term unit and plan how these services would be delivered.

A recurrent concern of the task force members in our weekly meeting was how we would provide thorough evaluative work-ups in a very short time. We assumed the length of stay would be less than one month for most of our prospective clients. In fact, we wanted to design programmatic components that could be fully implemented in less than two weeks.

The time frame presented a challenge for psychological and neurological testing. In order to provide a complete diagnostic and treatment-oriented assessment, the psychology department usually required several weeks to complete their battery of tests and generate the written summary report. The psychologist's written report was always of high quality, but our planning group feared it would do little good in terms of planning treatment if the psychological report arrived post-discharge. An additional concern was the fact there was often a long waiting list for psychological testing. We envisioned clients being referred for psychological testing on the day of their admission to the unit, but never actually being tested. This was not acceptable for a short-term, crisis intervention and evaluation unit.

I proposed using an art therapy assessment process, both as an initial evaluative procedure and as a mechanism for selecting clients who needed the full battery of psychological tests. My suggestion was warmly received, particularly when I said an art therapy assessment could be administered routinely within 48 hours of admission to the unit, and a complete written report made available to the treatment team within another 24 hours. The psychologist member of the task force expressed some concerns regarding art assessment procedures, but I assured her that in no way would art assessments duplicate psychological services, nor would art therapists violate the professional boundaries of another discipline.

With the endorsement of the short-term task force, my colleague Debra DeBrular and I began to review the existing art therapy assessment literature. Some of the assessment tools we considered seemed to be attempting to standardize artistic procedures. We did not think these assessment tools would be helpful in our setting because we didn't want to become "clever interpreters" (McNiff, 1981), nor did we wish to create a formulaic approach to image symbolism.

As we determined what we thought art therapy assessments should not be, we saw more clearly what we wanted them to be. First and foremost, we wanted to approach assessment as an on-going process, rather than as a one-time event. We wanted to provide the treatment team with an artistic and perhaps poetic portrait of the inner life of the person-in-crisis. Our hope was to design a process that would enable us to glimpse a candid snapshot of the psyche/soul. Rather than report standardized, measurable data, we sought to convey fleeting peeks at the interior worlds of children and adolescents.

In the early stages of our design process, we identified 11 aspects of art making. We theorized that these aspects would provide the art therapist with clues by which to construct a reliable, poetic narrative description of the client's sense of self, worldview, and relationships to others. These 11 aspects of art making were intended as an outline of the assessment process, not as a checklist evaluation. We had reservations about the use of checklists in mental health systems because checklists seem to reduce complex human beings, who happen to be clients, to convenient read-outs of observed behaviors. Our objection, on ethical and moral grounds, was that no human being should be reduced to dots, circles, or checks on computer data sheets or medical records database forms. We believed that attempts to summarize a person's strengths, weaknesses, motives, and struggles are best achieved through the concentrated effort of narrative form.

The Assessment Milieu and Process

The art therapy assessment process takes place in a small studio (Fig. 17). Clients are provided a work space and a range of media including: number 2 lead pencils, pens, colored pencils, crayons, craypas, oil stiks, charcoal, pastel chalks, watercolor paint sets, tempera paints and brushes, an assortment of drawing paper ranging in size from 8″ x 11″ through 28″ x 32″, assorted colors of construction paper, glue, scissors, modeling clay and miscellaneous found objects and wood scraps.

Three artistic tasks provide the structure of the assessment process: (1) Make whatever you would like to make; (2) Create an image of a good and bad memory; and (3) Make something with a bridge in it. We allot one hour for clients to complete the assessment process. The three artistic tasks are variations on procedures we had reviewed from art therapy literature. The first task, make whatever you would like to make, was a variation on the instruction in Ulman's (1965) Diagnostic Session, "Please use these materials to make a picture" (Ulman, 1992, p. 79). Our process, however, was not limited to making a picture. Our mentor, Don Jones, influenced the second task, to create an image of a good and bad memory. Don often reminded us to trust that whatever a client needs to express will be expressed. Along these lines, we thought that whatever memory images clients created would have potent meaning. An article by Hays and Lyons (1981) on the use of bridge drawings as a projective technique directly influenced the third drawing task of our assessment process.

In addition to our intentional design of the studio space, selection of media, and assignment of artistic tasks, we give attention to how the assessment process is introduced to the client. As the art therapist and client enter the studio, the art therapist gives an introduction and instructions that go something like this:

You are here for what is called an art therapy assessment. The purpose of this is to help us get a sense of how you see things in your life. We believe that people express themselves in many different ways. Some people are really good at talking about things, other people use poetry, or dance, or sports. During this session. you'll have a chance to express yourself through art.

In the time we have, about an hour or so, I'd like you to do three things. You can use any of the art materials in the room and I want you to know that whatever you do will be okay. The first thing I want you to do is to make whatever you'd like to make. It is absolutely up to you. The second task is to create an image, or images, of a good memory and a bad memory from your life. The third task is to create something that has a bridge in it.

My job here is to really pay attention. I want you to know that later today I will sit down with the things you have made and spend a couple of hours just looking at them and thinking about them. Then I will write a report and give it to your doctor. If you would like to read the report, your team will be glad to share it with you (Fig. 31).

After the instructions are given, the art therapist/assessor assumes a passive, observing stance. While the client engages in art making, the art therapist pays close attention to the following things.

Artistic Media. The first focal area was the client's selection and use of media. As stated above, a variety of media options with different material qualities were provided. The art therapist made note of the qualities of a particular media selected by the client. Ranges of media characteristics are considered, from resistive to pliable, controllable to fluid, familiar to unfamiliar, and requiring fine to gross motion movements.

Attentiveness to media characteristics and the client's selection process provide clues to understanding the client in conjunction with the other focal areas. In relation to media, we ask ourselves questions similar to these: *Given all of the media options available, what does it suggest when a client selects a #2 pencil and a small piece of drawing paper?*

Figure 31. An art assessment session in progress.

What might a client be expressing when he or she confines a drawing to only a small corner of the page? How is this different from the client who uses tempera paints and covers the largest paper available? These types of questions help us begin to formulate impressions of the client. We do not want to read too much into any one phenomenon; rather, we want to observe and collect as much information as possible.

Motion. The second area of attention was in relation to the motions used by the client during the assessment session. Ranges of motion characteristics are considered, from tight and constricted to loose and fluid, rhythmic to spasmodic, fine to gross, and aggressive to passive.

It is our sense that clients tend to utilize motions that are familiar. In an entirely non-verbal way, clients' movements offer hints about their style of interaction with the environment, how they cope with anxiety and how they relate to others.

Artistic Procedures. A third focal area is related to artistic procedures. We are curious about what clients might reveal about themselves through the procedural aspects of a freely chosen artistic task. Will the client choose artistic tasks requiring a degree of motor and mental coordination? Will the client choose tasks that involved a pronounced element of technical awareness, or will the client demonstrate a preference for simple, repetitive tasks? What is the client's level of procedural competence? Does the client invest in learning new skills in the midst of the session, or does he or she rely on familiar processes? The answers to these kinds of questions help us begin to understand the client's strengths in the assessment process.

Sexual Identification. The fourth focal area is sexual identification. We make note of the client's choice of media and tools, manner of implementation and interactive style, as well as the content of his or her artworks. While we do not want to engage in gender stereotyping, we do think it is important to pay attention to the cultural frame of reference in relation to sexual identification. We ask the following questions: Are any or all of these factors typically associated with masculinity or femininity? Is the artist's style of engagement with the task best described as passive, fine, intricate, or delicate? Is the artist's style aggressive, resistive, or rough?

The art therapy assessor is asked to factor in these observations in the context of the overall assessment process.

Self-Indulgence. The fifth area of focus is the degree of self-indulgence. Does the client appear to derive pleasure from the exhibitionistic aspect of the art process? Does she employ her own creative energy in the task or is her response mechanical and without pleasure? Does he value the end product and wish to take it with him, or does he abandon it without comment at the end of the session? Does the client appear to enjoy being observed by the art therapist, or is the art therapist's presence regarded as an intrusion or with indifference?

Dependence/Independence. The sixth area of attention is the range of dependent and/or independent action. Does the client appear to enjoy the nebulous instruction, "create whatever you want?" or does he demand, verbally or nonverbally, to be given more structure by the art therapy assessor? Does the client exhibit unique or individual performance? Does she identify with the end product as an expression of self? Are references made to her own body image or level of competencies?

Artistic Level of Development. The seventh focal area is that of artistic developmental level. We utilize Lowenfeld and Brittain's (1970) artistic developmental model because they are based on health rather than pathology. We believe this model provides the art therapy assessor with a normalized frame of reference.

Literal Description. The eighth aspect of attention is a literal exploration of what and how the client created. In this area of focus we attempt to pay attention to how things were made–the shapes, lines, forms, textures, and colors–without attaching any symbolic meaning.

Feeling Tone. The ninth focal area is that of the overall feeling tone of a given image. This aspect is dependent upon the art therapy assessor's ability to be open to the multiple feeling possibilities of the artwork, while simultaneously trusting his or her own subjective emotional response to the piece.

Symbolism. The tenth focal aspect we pay close attention to is the potential symbolism of clients' artworks, language, tone of voice, facial expressions, and body postures. In some ways, this is the most difficult of the focal areas since it clearly opens the door to evaluator projection and, as has already been mentioned, we do not embrace any formulas for interpretation. We think it is important to refrain from assigning particular fixed meanings to visual symbols. We do not want to commit imagicide. Still, one of the underlying principles of art therapy, that everything we create is a partial self-portrait implies that there is a wealth of information in the imaginative symbolic creations of the client. We rely on the subjective wisdom and compassion of the art therapy assessor. It is hoped that the symbols inherent in imagery, language, etc., when presented in the context of all the other focal areas, help to provide an accurate portrait of the client's inner world.

Subjective Response. The final area of focus in the art therapy assessment is the subjective response of the assessor. In attending to this aspect, the art therapist applies the discipline of looking, listening, and being with, in order to monitor his or her internal reactions to the client.

The art therapy assessment can be summarized as follows:
attention to media *plus*
attention to motion *plus*
attention to procedures *plus*
attention to sexual identification *plus*
attention to self indulgence *plus*
attention to dependence/independence *plus*
attention to artistic developmental level *plus*
attention to literal description *plus*
attention to feeling tone *plus*
attention to symbols *plus*
attention to subjective response
EQUALS the raw data of the narrative report.

Being open to–and paying attention to–these 11 aspects of artistic activity is not an easy process. All of the data gathered from the assessment session is considered as a whole, not in isolation. We look for repetition of data and themes. This form of art therapy assessment usually requires an hour to administer with the client. Additional time is needed to organize impressions of the data and outline the report. Writing the narrative account is also time intensive and demands good writing skills. Proper grammar, vocabulary, and sentence and paragraph construction skills are necessary. The assessor must not only be able to administer and organize the data, but must present it professionally, articulately, and compassionately.

After the client has completed the three artistic tasks, and after the art therapist has had time to reflect upon the artworks and the 11 focal aspects, it is time to write the narrative report.

The narrative format is outlined as follows:

I. Introduction

    A. identifying information regarding the client (age, gender, racial identity)

    B. description of the initial encounter between the client and the art therapist

    C. description of the client's general behavioral response to the assessment process

II. Reflection on the assessment session

    A. media

    B. motion

    C. artistic procedures

    D. sexual identification

    E. self-indulgence

    F. dependence/independence

    G. artistic level of development

    H. literal description

    I. feeling tone

    J. symbolism

    K. subjective response

III. Summary

    A. overview of the assessment

    B. implications for treatment

Narrative reports of art therapy assessments do not necessarily need to explicitly address each of the areas listed in the outline above. However, the outline serves as a helpful tool in organizing one's thoughts when writing the narrative. Below is an example of an art therapy assessment narrative report.

Art Therapy Assessment Narrative Report

Stephen _____

Introduction

Stephen _____, a 14-year-old caucasian male, was seen for an art therapy assessment interview on December 2, 1990. He presented himself as a pleasant, compliant, relatively easy-to-engage young man. He seemed fairly comfortable with the artistic tasks presented to him and he involved in the art processes enthusiastically. His movements, however, were rather tight and constricted throughout the interview.

As the art media were offered to him for use, Stephen was hesitant. He stated, "I'm not a good painter," and indicated he was unfamiliar with several of the other media available. After four or five minutes, he chose to work with a #2 lead pencil on an 18" x 24" piece of white paper. Despite his hesitancy in choosing art materials, he appeared to derive gratification from using what he described as, "such a big piece of paper." Three times he said, "I wish I could have paper like this to draw on at home." The abundance of supplies seemed to have positive meaning for him.

When given the opportunity to freely choose his subject matter for drawing, Stephen again hesitated. Several times I reassured him that whatever he chose to draw would be acceptable. After three to four minutes of silent inactivity, Stephen requested that I give him an idea. I encouraged Stephen to do whatever he would like to do. After several more minutes of inactivity, he appeared to be growing agitated and quite uncomfortable. Finally, he asked, "Would it be okay to draw a tree?"

I assured him that drawing a tree would be fine. He began to work immediately and seemed to relax within the structure of the session.

Reflection on the Assessment Process

When offered a variety of artistic materials, Stephen seemed to be overwhelmed. He was hesitant to utilize media with which he was unfamiliar. After several minutes of consideration, he chose to work with a standard #2 pencil on white paper. This may be significant in several ways: (1) the pencil is the most highly controllable of all the media options; (2) the pencil is the most common and familiar of the media; (3) the pencil is one of the most limited materials in relation to emotional expression in that it has no color; (4) pencil markings can be erased if perceived mistakes are made; (5) pencil is the least subject to accident or spontanaeity. When these media characteristics are considered in conjunction with Stephen's tight and constricted range of motion, one begins to sense a quality of inhibition or tentativeness.

For his free choice image Stephen created an intriguing drawing of a tree. He said the tree was a big hickory. In fact, his drawing of it was too large to be contained by the paper. He said, "This tree reminds me of one that's in the field by my house." He portrayed a large, sturdy trunk that extended off the page. In artistic terms, this is referred to as breaking the plane of the drawing.

A network of branches emerged approximately halfway up the trunk. Just below the branch system, he drew a thick poison ivy vine that wraped around the trunk. Stephen devoted much time and energy to realistically rendering the branches and the poison ivy. Where the base of the trunk met the ground, however, was drawn in a minimalist and stylized fashion. The ground line was depicted with a single wavy line, roughly three inches above the bottom of the page.

Perhaps it is significant that the ground line did not extend from edge to edge on the paper. This was in contrast to both the trunk and the branch network, which each extended off the page. Literally speaking, ground is the base for trees in the world. Stephen's minimalist handling of the ground line may indicate his foundation is not secure. The sense that Stephen has no solid foundation is further suggested by the absence of any visual references to a root system. When commenting upon this, Stephen said, "I guess there are no roots."

Stephen's artistic style is fairly advanced but appropriate for his chronological age. He drew with a measure of technical skill. In looking at his style of application of pencil to paper, one is struck by the effort and clarity with which he portrayed the branches and ivy when contrasted with the very light, faint, and sketchy handling of the lower trunk and ground surface.

It is interesting that he drew a complex system of thick, solid-looking limbs and myriad twig-like smaller branches. There were more than one hundred of these small, carefully detailed branches.

The tree was depicted standing by itself in an open field. No other trees were in view and no other life forms were shown. The emotional tone of the image conveyed a sense of independence, loneliness, isolation, and abandonment.

There were many potential symbols present in this drawing. One may certainly view Stephen's attention to detail in the branches as indicative of his interest in reaching out into the world. The branch system dominated his use of time and clearly was the area of most interest to him. The image was complicated, suggesting that the appropriate developmental task of reaching outward toward others, particularly peers, is a complex yet crucial matter for him.

The trunk of the tree was paradoxical. On the one hand, it appeared to be a strong, thick trunk, while on the other hand, he drew it in a sketchy and tentative manner, particularly where it met the ground line. In addition, the trunk was encircled by poison ivy. Regarding this area of his drawing, Stephen commented, "The poison ivy appears to be suffocating it." In addition, there was no root system portrayed and the trunk appeared to fade into the ground. In literature, poetry, and art, roots tend to represent nourishment and attachment. This image suggests qualities of detachment and malnourishment.

As he worked, Stephen spontaneously associated this tree with the cultural reference, a family tree. He mentioned a number of different people in his immediate and extended family. Through the telling of several vignettes, he communicated his belief that his family has always regarded him as "defective." He stated that his parents used to say he had "spells" that they referred to as "fits and fevers." Other vignettes he shared revolved around what he described as "funny things" that happened at family reunions when everybody drank too much.

Stephen also spoke of times when he was in the presence of the real tree his drawing represented. He shared warm feelings and memories of playing on or around the tree when he was a child. He indicated that these were usually times when he was by himself and happy.

The recurrent metaphoric themes connected with this image seem to be four-fold. The first was the sketchy, faint manner in which the tree was connected (or not connected) with the ground. This seems to indicate a sense of detachment and may suggest feelings of abandonment. Second, the poison ivy wrapped around the tree brings to mind his sense of being *damaged* or *defective*. Third, the branch system, toward which he exerted such focused effort drawing, may represent the interest and energy Stephen employs in his attempts to connect with others. Finally, the tree was drawn in the season of winter. There were no leaves shown at all and one was left, when looking at it, with a sense of bleak sadness and loneliness.

For his second artistic task, Stephen was asked to create an image of a good and bad memory. He chose to use tempera paints and a 28″ x 32″ sheet of tag board for this exercise. Tempera paint is a medium that easily lends itself to emotional expression. Tempera is more fluid than pencil but still relatively easy to control. It was evident by the ease with which he applied the paint that Stephen had used this medium before.

Stephen employed a thick paintbrush and black paint to divide the tag board in half. He quickly covered the entire left side with solid black, and the right side with red. He worked very intensely on covering the entire white surface. Stephen said, "The black side is my bad memory. The red side is the good memory."

I asked if he would like to tell the story of the black and red.

He responded, "There isn't much to tell. The bad memory is my when my mom was killed in a car accident. The good memory is from when my baseball team won the league." As Stephen spoke of his memories, he would not establish eye contact with me. His voice was quiet, nearly inaudible.

"Do you want to say anything more about these images? I asked.

"No," he said.

For the third artistic task, Stephen was asked to create a bridge. He appeared rather preoccupied and/or disinterested in this task. It was my sense that the memory images had raised uncomfortable feelings for him and this perhaps precluded focused attention on the bridge image.

After a couple of minutes' thought, Stephen used an 18″ x 11″ piece of black construction paper to roll a cylinder. He then crumpled the cylinder and bent it into the form of an arch. He taped the ends of the arch to the worktable, sat back and said, "There, that's it."

"Can you say anything about your bridge?" I asked.

"Not a very safe bridge," he replied.

I asked, "What does the bridge cross over?"

"I'm not sure . . . a raging river I guess. Can I go back to the unit now?

Summary

Stephen presents himself as a young man who is pleasant, yet depressed and isolated. He possesses above average drawing skills, which is an area of strength. He is particularly adept in visual abstract processing. However, it was apparent that his intense feelings get in the way of his ability to stay focused on tasks. This suggests that his underlying feelings of sadness and abandonment disrupt his ability to function at age-appropriate life tasks.

In relation to his treatment, it will be important for caregivers to pay attention to Stephen's socialization efforts with peers. The branch network in his tree drawing suggests that his efforts to reach out to others, to connect with others, are of great importance to him. This is particularly poignant given the tragic death of his mother. He may benefit from therapeutic activities that promote the development of communication and relating skills. While he may appear pleasant and competent, therapists must remain aware of his perception of himself as being damaged.

An area of strength for Stephen is his ability to work in a concentrated manner for a period of time. He was able to stay on task and work intently for 40 minutes on his tree drawing. This suggests a capacity to focus in areas that interest him, when he is not overwhelmed with sadness.

For successful treatment to occur, it will be imperative that attention be given to his view of the family. The vignettes he shared regarding family interactions and his sense of place in the family indicate problematic relating styles. The loss of his mother seems to be a major trauma that has yet to be worked through.

Therapists will also want to give attention to Stephen's areas of strength. He may benefit from therapeutic groups that allow for expression of feelings through action. Visual tasks and other related activities might be gratifying to him. Such activities, in the service of self-expression and development of relationships, may also serve to loosen his constricted movement style and build his sense of competence and mastery in the world. These experiences will be given additional meaning if Stephen receives validation from significant others.

It is my sense that Stephen sees his world as a lonely and rather hazardous place. His bridge construction suggests feelings of danger, inadequacy and hopelessness. He seems emotionally adrift, hurting and confused at this time. Therapists are advised to keep in mind the metaphors of a tree without roots and a poorly constructed bridge over a raging river. These images capture the essence of Stephen's view of the world. As caregivers, we need to help him grow roots and construct guardrails.

BRUCE L. MOON, ATR-BC

Art therapy assessment narrative reports can offer treatment teams a unique view of the client, but it is important to note that assessment is a process, not an event. By this, I mean that assessment is an ongoing phenomenon in the context of art therapy relationships. People are continually growing and changing. It would be a fallacy to presume that an art therapy assessment report can capture the dynamic nature of a living person. The assessment report is by nature static: people are seldom so. This is why it is important to write assessment reports utilizing language that is compassionate and creative, while at the same time being accurate, descriptive, and professional.

Chapter XXI

THE ROLE OF WORK

The Twenty-First Essential–Art therapists have a profound respect for the *work* of art, the *work* of the client, and the *work* of the therapist.

The farmer plows the earth, he harrows it, tears it, pulverizes it; he pulls out weeds, or cuts them, or burns them; he poisons insects, and fights against drought and floods. To be sure, all of this is done in order to create something, for which reason we can call it work and not rage.
Karl Menninger, 1970, p. 134

Karl Menninger's (1970) description of the farmer could easily be applied to the ceramicist who pounds and kneads clay, or the metalsmith who melts and pours metal into the mold, or the sculptor who chisels stone. In each case, the same destructive force is used for the constructive purpose of "work and not rage."

Even the computer programmer, the teacher, and the carpenter share the urge to master. The computer programmer seeks to organize, reformulate, and control data. The teacher directs, shapes, and molds the intellectual growth of her students. The carpenter saws, nails, and fits each piece of wood in order to build the house. In each case, we grasp the underlying impulse to assert mastery over the environment.

It is no coincidence that *work* is often closely associated with the arts. When an artist's exhibit opens, the objects are described as *works of art.* They are not advertised as *plays of art.* They are works of art. It is curious that in our current cultural viewpoint the arts are sometimes considered frivolous (Ewens, 1988). In our public education system, the arts are often the first targets of budget cuts and are almost never offered on a daily basis, as are mathematics and sciences. The arts have come to be viewed as something one does in leisure time, rather than as one's work.

Art therapy students bring to the educational setting a long history, both personal and cultural, of a paradoxical understanding of art. On the one hand, art is revered and displayed in multi-million dollar museums. On the other hand, art is regarded as frivolous, as an unnecessary frill. This presents a peculiar dilemma for the art therapy educator who must help students to rediscover the *work* of art in order to enable the student to ennoble the work of the artist-client and the artist-therapist.

Clients do not come to art therapy in order to engage in frills-therapy. The client comes to work on intrapsychic, physical, or interpersonal difficulties. The art therapist, regardless of how benevolent her intention, who views the arts as anything less than the noble transformation of inner energy into constructive external ends, may inadvertently fail the client. Such an art therapist will fail to grasp the depth and significance of the work that lies ahead of the client. The work of being in art therapy may be trivialized and the client will ultimately be frustrated by the futility of his or her struggle. In art therapy encounters, the art therapists' work is to help clients transform energy. This is hard work, neither trivial nor frilly.

In preparing art therapists, it is essential to engender a profound respect for the *work* of art, the *work* of the client, and of the *work* of the therapist. The drive toward mastery is a strong motivation in each of these three aspects of the work. The sense of competence derived from mastery of complicated problems is directly linked to self-discipline, which eventuates in pleasure. From mastery and self-discipline, there grows what I describe as a sacred passion for life. It is marked by an authentic, creative, and vital relationship between the individual and the world. The artist's use of media in a masterful way is a creative and vital relationship experience, but technical skill is empty without the emotional investment of the artist. The success of an artwork depends equally on its communication of feeling and its demonstration of competent handling of materials.

The success or failure of an art therapist's work with a client cannot be based solely upon the temporary cathartic expressions of the client. Consideration of the development of formal artistic skills can also be a factor in evaluating the quality of an art therapist's work. In art ther-

Figure 32. It is essential to engender a profound respect for the work.

apy education, there must be careful attention given to ongoing development of expertise with artistic processes, hand in hand with relationship skills, communication skills, and therapeutic techniques.

In a profound sense, mastery of artistic process may be viewed as the capacity to organize and transform experience. When the capacity to organize and transform experience is coupled with respect for the nature of artistic work, we begin to glimpse the significance that art making can manifest in therapeutic processes. Engagement in art tasks provides a therapeutic context through which powerful destructive forces are transformed into constructive, meaningful objects. A swirling mix of feelings, thoughts, sensations, actions, and relationships are often markers of emotional and mental distress. Art making can help to organize chaotic thoughts and emotional experiences and give the artist-client a coherent, reorganized product. Metaverbally, the art making serves to alleviate distress through the work (the activity) itself and thus provides hope for clarity and balance.

As a client's sense of competence builds in relation to a particular artistic task, there is invariably a corresponding increase in self-esteem and confidence. This establishes a form of reciprocity among artist/client, art process, and art product that is contagious. As the client grows in her ability to handle art materials masterfully, the ability to handle other aspects of her life grows as well, and vice-versa.

I am obliged to caution the reader that technical competence alone will not alleviate the distress or erase the dysfunction of the client. If that were the case, there would be no need for arts therapists. My intent here is to highlight one specific aspect of the prismatic nature of the art therapy profession that, in my view, has too often been forsaken in pursuit of expression. Expression and skill are essential to one another, just as tragedy and opportunity, according to the Chinese proverb, different sides of the same coin.

Over the past several decades, our societal regard for the notion of *work* has undergone an intriguing schism. Many people view their work as drudgery that must be endured for 40 hours a week. It is as if work is the sentence for the crime of growing up. A popular country ballad poeticized this sentiment: "Take this job and shove it" (Paycheck, 1996).

The workaholic, the person who cannot separate himself from his work, who is in essence addicted to the job, embodies another view of work. These are the individuals who log 60, 70, or more hours on the job each week. They eat, sleep, and breathe their work because there is little else to give their lives meaning.

A third view of work comes from a hedonistic perspective wherein work is regarded purely as a means to an end, the end being material gain. People who regard their work in this way measure the meaning of their lives by the number of things they own.

It is important for art therapists to manifest a well-balanced and positive view of their work. The notion that actions speak louder than words suggests that what we *do* is who we *are*. For many of us, a significant portion of our lives is spent doing work. Work defines who we are.

It is tragic that so many people define themselves as prisoners, addicts or hedonists. Art therapy students, having lived in this society, may bring to the educational setting one of these views of work. It is essential that art therapy educators be attentive to these possible views of work their students may manifest. By focusing on an artistic understanding of work, i.e., as a noble transformation of inner energy into constructive external ends, educational programs can do much to help the student develop a healthy perspective.

The development of a healthy, balanced, and meaning-filled attitude toward work cannot simply be taught; the teacher, mentor, and supervisor must model it. Failing to do this will have an effect upon the art therapy student's future clients. The art therapist who views her work as drudgery cannot help her client be freed from emotional incarceration. Likewise, the art therapist who is overly committed and addicted to her work will no doubt leak her compulsion into the therapy milieu. And the art therapist who is overly concerned with her own material gain will find it nearly impossible to discover meaning in the broken, ruined, or impoverished aspects of the client's self-image. For the good of art therapy students and all future clients, it is essential that positive values regarding the nature of work be fostered and nourished in art therapy educational programs.

Chapter XXII

PAINTING MY WAY HOME

The Twenty-Second Essential—The art therapy process is about knowing when and how to immerse oneself in the creative flow.

For many years I made art alongside students. In 1991, I was teaching a course titled Studio Methods Seminar. Its purpose was to give students time in the creative arts studio to make art for themselves, without the burden and distractions of client-related responsibilities. I wanted the students to focus on creative self-exploration and to learn the professional value of sustaining their own artistic development. In this seminar, students were provided with an opportunity to integrate, through artistic processes, the wide range of academic, clinical, and emotional experiences inherent in graduate art therapy study. The core expectation was that each student would work on major artistic pieces in an effort to creatively document his or her educational experience. Students were encouraged to paint, sculpt, make collage, or use any other media that involved prolonged engagement. The process and subject matter of the artworks became a focus of discussion in the class sessions. In addition, there were other less observable, subtler objectives.

Several years ago, my wife Cathy and I built a 2,000 square foot log cabin. It is safe to say that nearly every piece of wood in the house bears our fingerprints. I recall many instances during the active construction when my children, aged three and six at the time, would sit and watch what we were doing. At the time, I thought they were hungry for parental attention and so stayed close to us. While that was surely true, I have thought since that they were engaged in a research task. They were studying Mom and Dad, making careful mental notes about what it was to be a man and a woman, to be in relationship, to work hard, and to create something as large as a house.

In post-industrial America, the opportunities for such an extended laboratory experience of watching parents work together is rare for children. In the 1940s, fathers dropped out of their children's view. Fathers went to work, stayed there for eight to 12 hours, and came home tired. The economic and lifestyle pressures of the 1970s and 80s extended this phenomenon to mothers as well. The stay-at-home housewife/mother is now a minority.

Our children learned many life lessons watching Cathy and me. They learned in a way that children have done for most of humankind's history, through direct observation and participation. Robert Bly (1990) writes of the absence of such experiences, "Throughout the ancient hunter societies, which apparently lasted thousands of years—perhaps hundreds of thousands—and throughout the hunter-gatherer societies that followed them, and the subsequent agricultural and craft societies, fathers and sons worked and lived together (p. 95). Bly adds that not seeing the father when the child is small, never being with him, having a remote father is an injury. Bly encourages men to re-engage in initiatory experiences between the generations. In primitive societies, boys and girls become men and women only through ritual, effort, and only with the active involvement of older men and women. I believe this is true of the world of the art therapist as well. Women and men do not become art therapists without the initiatory involvement of art therapy mentors.

The hours I spend in art studios with students are initiatory ritual time. Students do not enter the world of the art therapist simply by taking the right courses. The active involvement and intervention of mentors is essential. This means that seasoned practitioners welcome and initiate the novice who is entering the mythologized, mysterious, and intuitive world of art therapy.

I regard initiating art therapy students into the profession as sacred work. Each time a student baptizes her wounds with paint or chalk, she receives the nourishment and courage her journey requires. Initiation into this work is a process of helping students know when and how to become immersed in the creative flow.

There are many unspoken benefits for my students (and me) that come from this initiatory rite. I do not have to tell my students I believe in the power of the creative process. They see my faith with their own eyes. I do not have to talk about my belief in the importance of art therapists' ongoing involvement in personal art making, for they experience my commitment. Students do not have to wander fearfully and alone through their artistic journey, because I travel with them and they are welcomed into the ritual of artistic self-exploration. By working in the studio together we engage in initiatory rituals.

Ritual in Progress

In April of 1991 I began a painting (Fig. 33) in Studio Methods Seminar. I started by painting the entire canvas a light, greenish blue. This was rather odd for me, because at that time I seldom used pastel colors and only occasionally worked with cool colors. My students remarked that this was an "out of character" start. Regardless, something in the color seemed to call to me and I responded. Then, having a solid pastel, blue-green background, I began to work on an image of a table. I had no formal plan for this painting. I simply let it lead me where it wanted to go. When I finished the base color for the table, it

Figure 33. The hours I spend in art studios with students are initiatory ritual time.

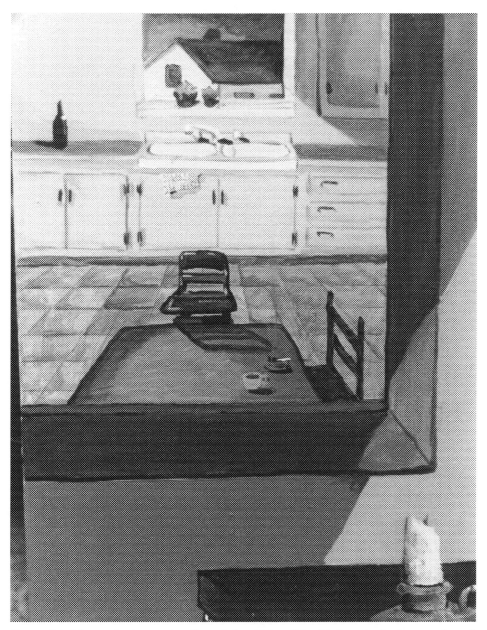

Figure 34. I knew the image it reflected should be of the kitchen in the house where I grew up.

Figure 35. My father shortly before his death.

looked dark and heavy against the light background. The heaviness made me feel uncomfortable. I didn't want to look at it. When I returned to the studio the following week, I was again repelled by the darkness of the table. I decided to paint a soft printed cloth covering part of the table. The image of a flowered table runner presented itself to my mind's eye and I added it to the painting.

As I was working on this section, I began thinking about my mother's house. My mother was 80 years old at the time and her house was filled with soft things–doilies and memorabilia of children, grandchildren, and great-grandchildren. During this period of reflection, it occurred to me that the painting might be a sort of nostalgia image. I decided to hang (paint) a mirror on the upper left section of the canvas to emphasize this reflecting.

The moment I began to paint the frame of the mirror, I knew the image it reflected should be of the kitchen in the house where I grew up (Fig. 34). Suddenly the initial background color made sense.

"It's aqua," I said. My students looked at me with puzzlement.

"It's aqua. My sisters and I used to give my mom a hard time about always painting her kitchen the same color . . . aqua!"

The images in the mirror came quickly. The old porcelain sink, a dishrag hanging on the cabinet door. Violets on the windowsill. A circular fluorescent light glaring from the ceiling. Kitchen table, cup of coffee, lit Chesterfield cigarette. These images are burned deeply into my childhood memory.

At some point, one of the students asked if I planned to paint a portrait of my mother standing in the kitchen. I said I wasn't sure, but something moved deep in the pit of my stomach as I answered.

I decided to focus on the table and avoid the kitchen for a time. Again, the images presented themselves quickly. I painted a candle and holder, but was undecided as to whether to paint a flame on the wick of the candle or not. I painted a picture frame containing a portrait of my father as a young man. It portrayed him as a baseball catcher about to catch a fastball.

A week went by. When I returned to the studio the image of my father felt wrong. It's hard to describe. I just knew it was wrong. I painted over that section in white. Now the image of my father as a 44-year-old man (shortly before his death) emerged (Fig. 35). This time the image felt good.

One of my students commented, "Well, if you're going to have your dad in there, I think you'd better put your mother in the mirror." Again I was confronted with the issue.

The Studio Methods Seminar class met every Wednesday afternoon from 3:30 till 5:00. On the Tuesday before the next session, July 16, I received an emergency telephone call from my sister informing me that our mother had had a serious stroke. Her physician wanted the immediate family to gather to discuss treatment options.

Over the next four weeks, my mother endured paralysis and was unable to speak. When her physical condition stabilized, she was transferred to a nursing home. She died on August 18, 1991.

As I entered the studio and looked at my nearly completed painting, its messages were clear and strong. This painting was a preparation of sorts for my mother's death. My struggle with whether or not to include her in the piece was an intuitive, painful ritual of transition for me. I recognized that I was now no one's son. I had no parents. One of the students, Arlene Weiss, said to me, "You are a grown up orphan."

Yes.

The painting knew. I signed it on Wednesday, August 26, the ritual complete. My students watched this. They traveled with me. They could not have doubted that I believe in what I was doing. They saw me dip my wounds in paint and draw the nourishment and strength I needed to continue my journey.

They watched as I painted my way home.

I welcomed them.

EPILOGUE

Our journey together is nearly complete. We have traveled a path bordered by images of mastery, beginning, chaos and order, and love. I have focused on significant themes that emerge in the educational journey. Among these themes are the importance of the relationship between art therapy students and their mentors and supervisors, the role of art making in art therapy education, and art's place in the core curriculum and practicum sites. I believe that the work of art therapy has to do with science, soul, and creative process and I have addressed these areas within the text.

I hope that through it all you have sensed the deep respect and passion I feel for art therapy students and the art therapy profession. There is really nothing I would rather do with my life than to be an art therapist. When I was in training with Don Jones, he would often say, "Blessed is the man who can't tell the difference between his vocation and his avocation." I agree, and I have been blessed.

In this second edition of *Essentials of Art Therapy Education and Practice*, I have tried to present important aspects of art therapy education. We art therapists and educators truly do good work and I believe the world is a better place because of our efforts. As the art therapy profession continues to grow and evolve, it is my strongest desire that we stay true to our artistic roots.

Whether you are a teacher, student, or art therapy practitioner, I urge you to always keep the wonder, the mystery, and the love of art before you and within you. Yes.

BRUCE L. MOON, Mundelein, IL, July 2002

REFERENCES

Allen, P. (1992). Artist in residence: An alternative to "clinification" for art therapists. *Art Therapy: Journal of the American Art Therapy Association, 9*, 22–28.

Allen, P. (1994). Soul and spirit. *Art Therapy: Journal of the American Art Therapy Association, 11*, 17–18.

Allen, P. (1995). *Art is a way of knowing.* Boston: Shambhala.

Berry, W. (1990). *What are people for?* Berkeley, CA: North Point.

Bly, R. (1990). *Iron John.* New York: Addison-Wesley.

Campbell, J. (1988). *The power of myth.* New York: Doubleday.

Chowdorow, N. (1978). *The reproduction of mothering.* Berkley, CA: University of California Press.

DeBrular, D., & Moon, B. (1989). *Precious gifts.* Proceedings of the 20th Annual Conference of the American Art Therapy Association. AATA Author.

Ewens, T. (1988). Flawed understandings: On Getty, Eisner and DBAE. In J. Burton, A. Lederman, & P. London (eds.) *Beyond DBAE: The case for multiple visions of art education.* North Dartmouth, MA: Southeastern Massachusetts University.

Feder, E., & Feder, B. (1981). *Expressive arts therapies.* Englewood Cliffs, NJ: Prentice-Hall.

Frankl, V. (1969). *Man's search for meaning: An introduction to logotherapy.* Philadelphia: Washington Square Press.

Gilligan, C. (1982). *In a different voice.* Cambridge, MA: Harvard University Press.

Hays, R. & Lyons, S. (1981). The bridge drawing: A projective technique for assessment in art therapy. *The Arts in Psychotherapy, 8*, 207–217.

Hillman, J. (1989). *A blue fire.* New York: Harper & Row.

Hillman, J. (1977). *Re-visioning psychology.* New York: Harper Collins.

Janson, H.W. (1973). *History of art.* New York: Prentice Hall.

Jordan, J. (1986). *Relational development: Therapeutic implication of empathy and shame.* New York: The Stone Center.

Kafka, F. (1930). *The castle.* New York: Alfred A. Knopf.

Kierkegaard, S. (1956). *Purity of heart.* New York: Harper.

Lowenfeld, V., & Brittain, W.L. (1970). *Creative and mental growth* (5th ed.). New York: Macmillan.

McNiff, S. (1981). *The arts and psychotherapy.* Springfield, IL: Charles C Thomas.

McNiff, S. (1989). *Depth psychology of art.* Springfield, IL: Charles C Thomas.

McNiff, S. (1991). Ethics and the autonomy of images. *The Arts in Psychotherapy, 18.*

Menninger, K. A. (1970). *Love against hate.* New York: Harcourt, Brace & World.

Membership survey of the American Art Therapy Association. (1998). AATA, Editor.

Miller, J. B. (1987). *Toward a new psychology of women.* Boston: Beacon Press.

Moon, B. (1990, 1995). *Existential art therapy: The canvas mirror.* Springfield, IL: Charles C Thomas.

Moon, B. (1997). *Welcome to the studio: The role of responsive art making in art therapy.* Unpublished Dissertation.

Moon, C. (1988). *Words beyond words: Articulation of the art therapy experience.* Proceedings of the 19th Annual Conference of the American Art Therapy Association, p. 103.

Nelson, J. (1985). *Male sexuality and masculine spirituality.* The Sex Information and Education Council of the United States Report, Vol. XIII Number 4. New York.

Papini, G. (1969). A visit to Freud. Reprinted in *Review of Existential Psychology and Psychiatry, 9,* 2.

Paycheck, J. (1996). Take this job and shove it. *The best of Johnny Paycheck,* CD. Nashville: Curb Records.

Peck, S. (1978). *The road less traveled.* New York: Simon and Schuster.

Robbins, A. (1988). A psychoaesthetic perspective on creative arts therapy and training. *The Arts in Psychotherapy, 15,* 95–100.

Rubin, J. (1984). *The art of art therapy.* New York: Brunner Mazel.

Samuels, M., & Samuels, N. (1975). *Seeing with the mind's eye: The history, techniques and uses of visualization.* New York: Random House.

Sillitoe, A. (1959). *The loneliness of a long distance runner.* New York: Signet/New American Library.

Simon, P. (1965). I am a rock. *Sounds of silence,* LP. New York: Eclectic Music.

Teall, E. N. (Ed.). (1984). *New concise Webster's dictionary.* New York: Modern Publishing.

Ulman, E. (1965). Creativity for the exceptional individual. *Bulletin of Art Therapy, 4,* 91–116.

Ulman, E. (1992). A new use of art in psychiatric diagnosis. *American Journal of Art Therapy, 30,* 79. Montpelier, VT: Vermont College of Norwich University.

Wadeson, H. (1980). *Art psychotherapy.* New York: John Wiley.

(1998). *Webster's new world dictionary: Third college ed.* New York: Simon and Schuster, Inc.

Whyte, D. (1990). *Where many rivers meet.* Langley, WA: Many Rivers Press.

Yalom, I. (1995). *The theory and practice of group psychotherapy.* New York: Basic Books.

INDEX

A

American Art Therapy Association, ix, 54,
    66, 93, 99
AATA Educational Standards, 61, 67, 68
Allen, Pat B., 11, 18
American Journal of Art Therapy, 59
Art Experience, 53–58
Art Making, 11–19
Arts in Psychotherapy, 59
Assessment, 77, 148–162

B

Barlowe, Gary, 66
Bly, Robert, 63, 169
Burke, Sr. Kathleen, 77

C

Cain, Jerllee, 5
Campbell, Joseph, 63, 81, 82
Camus, Albert, 63
Castle, the, 46
Chaos, 30–36
Chowdorow, Nancy, 97, 100
Clinical Art Therapy Graduate Intensive, 4
Columbus College of Art and Design, 22
Confidentiality, 90
Core curriculum, 59–65

D

DeBrular, Deb, xi, 90, 93–107, 149
Depth Psychology of Art, 56
Devotional Seeing, 8
Donne, John, 63
Dulicai, Diane, 114

E

Empathic confrontation, 50
Existential Art Therapy, 110, 113, 130
Existentialism, 113

F

Failure, 131–136
Fear, 47
Feder, Elaine, 62
Feder, Bernard, 62
Freud, Sigmund, 83
Frost, Robert, 63

G

Grimm's Fairy Tales, 63
Gilligan, Carol, 150
Gibbs, George, 131

H

Harding Hospital, 6, 45
Hays, Ronald, 150
Healer, 50
Hero, 37–41
Hillman, James, 3, 78
Holidays, 117–121
Hopper, Edward, 5
Huestis, Robert, 108

I

Identity as an artist, 11–19, 53–58
Image, 3–10
Imagicide, 4
Intrusion, 101
It, The story of, 20–21

J

Janson, H.W., 4
Jones, Don, 54, 59, 93, 150, 175
Jordan, Judith, 100
Journal of the American Art Therapy
    Association, 59
Journey, 37–41

K

Kafka, Franz, 46
King, Stephen, 63
Kinsella, W.P., 63
Kierkegaard, Soren, 8

L

Lantz, Jim, v
Lawrence, D.H., 63
Lebeiko, Carol, 111
Lesley University, 81
Leuchter, Henry, 136
Loneliness of a Long Distance Runner, 96
Love, 142–147

M

Masculine spirituality, 96–97
McNiff, Shaun, 4, 56, 77, 130, 141, 149
Melville, Herman, 63
Menninger, Karl, 163
Mentor, 42–52
Metaphor, 51, 137–141, 159
Metaverbal, 13, 91, 122–129
Methodist Theological School in Ohio, 66
Michaelangelo, 82
Miller, Jean Baker, 100
Moon, Catherine, 7, 126, 168, 169

N

Nietzsche, Friederich, 116, 128
Nelson, James, 96
Nighthawks, 5
Nolan, Paul, 114

O

Observing ego, 49

P

Painting, 168–174
Papini, Giovanni, 83
Passions, 84
Paycheck, Johnny, 166
Paxton, Tom, 87
Peck, M. Scott, 142
Philosophy, 108–116
Powers, Mary Lou, 11, 22–29, 81
Precious Gifts, 99–102
Projection, 7
Psyche, 61

R

Rice, A.K., 93
Ritual, 170–174
Robbins, Arthur, 29
Rubin, Judith, 82

S

Sallinger, J.D., 63
Science, 7–80
Selle, Joan, 86, 88
Sexuality, 49
Sillitoe, Allan, 96
Simon, Paul, 142
Soul, 16, 61, 77–80
Spirituality, 16–17
Studio Methods Seminar, 168–174

T

Tavistock, 93
Teamwork, 114–116
Therapy, 61

U

Ulman, Elinor, 150
Ursuline College, 77

V

Veri, Darienne, 39
Vonnegut, Kurt, 63

Y

Yalum, I., 12

W

Wadeson, Harriet, 59
Weiss, Arlene, 174
Whyte, David, 3, 6
Work, , 163–167
Worthington Community Counseling
    Service, 66
Wright State University, 66

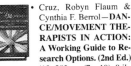

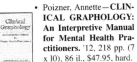

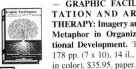
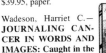